ISLAM

God's Forgotten Blessing

Stephen Dickie

Acknowledgements

This publication could not have been possible without the untiring efforts of Malachi, Jack, Ken and Steven–my walking Arabic dictionary.

The prayers and support of friend and fellow researcher, Rudy, made this book possible. When we came up to an unknown, not knowing how to proceed, the Holy Spirit would direct us to the needed information again and again.

To my faithful wife who has encouraged and supported me as this book took on a life of its own.

To my friend Ed who did so many things for the ministry that gave me more time to spend on this work.

The insight given to me by Elder Robert Darnell, who I only met through his recorded sermons on Islam, was the catalyst that revealed to me the other side of the "children of the East" that I had never known existed. Elder Darnell went to his rest in 1996 and is awaiting the resurrection.

To Vicki Lawrence, who supplied the jots and tittles that I never knew were needed for a work like this—thank you from the bottom of my heart.

My people are destroyed for lack of knowledge: because thou hast rejected knowledge, I will also reject thee, that thou shalt be no priest to me: seeing thou hast forgotten the law of thy God, I will also forget thy children.
Hosea 4:6

Contents

Foreword   6

Introduction   8

Chapter:

1 An Eye-Opening Tour   11

2 Silk Highways—Detained—Plan for Central Asia   16

3 Information Search Begins, But Where?   20

4 The Bible and Islam   25

5 The Search for More Information   35

6 Revelation 9:1 Considered   39

7 What is Biblical Smoke?   47

8 The Seal of God   53

9 Scorpions, Locusts, Horses and Lions   59

10 Sixth Trumpet–Second Woe   64

11 Application of the Second Woe   73

12 Seventh Trumpet-Third Woe Relation to Third Angel   84

13 What Will Be?   90

14 Time of the Remnant   95

15 Central Asia Evangelism Experiment   105

16 People Stories of the Meetings   112

17 Is There Another Way to Reach Our Brothers and Sisters,
    the "Children of the East?"   125

Author's Notes   132

2300-Day Time Line   134

Maps   137

Foreword

Islam, God's Forgotten Blessing presents one of the timeliest and urgent challenges facing God's people today.

Before Jesus ascended, He told His disciples to go and give the gospel invitation to all people everywhere, and they did. The apostles and early church evangelists circled the globe to reach the Jewish and pagan people of the planet with the good news of salvation.

Before Jesus returns, He said that the conclusive sign announcing the nearness of His coming would again be the giving of the gospel to every national, indigenous, cultural and linguistic group living on the earth at the end of time. At present, this mission is rapidly progressing toward a climax.

Our strategy for Global Mission to "Tell the World Now" will, of necessity, include reaching all the sons of Abraham, Jews and Muslims alike, with the exciting news about the soon, sudden and surprising return of Jesus to establish His universal kingdom of glory.

However, in accepting this colossal challenge we are to include the multiplied millions of each Islamic sect which together totals more than one billion worldwide.

Today, Muslims live in most of the nations of our modern world. We see them as physicians, surgeons, university professors, attorneys, corporate owners, developers, investment bankers, merchants, as well as those from ordinary walks of life, and they are virtually unnoticed.

Muslims are people just as we are who love their families and their homes. They integrate well into their local society and live within many different cultures. Muslims are basically a happy, wholesome, and productive people and may be your neighbors.

Unfortunately, to a large degree, Muslims are greatly misunderstood. Most of them are modest, mild-mannered persons who are not fanatical or extremist. They are also sincere seekers of God's will for their lives, even more than many Christians.

We should remember that Christians and Muslims worship and serve the same God, the God of Abraham. In addition, it may be surprising to learn that the remnant of Bible-believing Christians living today and the remnant of genuine Muslims found around the world have more in common than perhaps either group may recognize.

This book, Islam, God's Forgotten Blessing, gives insight and information about the traditions and teachings of Islam and how we may introduce Muslims to the real Jesus of the Bible.

God's Holy Spirit is speaking directly to the hearts of honest and sincere Muslims just as much as anyone else who seeks after God. We must never forget that salvation is inclusive of all racial, cultural, national, and religious groups and God does not discriminate.

The Bible teaches that God loves all people, of all classes, of all races, of all nations, of all times, and is not willing that any should perish. Let us also recognize the wonderful fact that God loves Muslims, too!

Fortunately, the fanatics and extremists of Islam, like the fanatics and extremists of Christianity, Judaism, and all other religious faiths, are actually a small minority by comparison. Praise God, Jesus died for every single person who has ever lived in this world of sin and rebellion against God.

Today God is calling all Muslims, just as He is calling all people from the vast number of climes, cultures and isms on the face of the earth to be ready for Christ's coming kingdom.

I fully believe there will be millions of Muslims, who, with all the people of God around the world, will respond to God's final call and quickly prepare for the soon coming of our Lord and Savior, Jesus Christ!

— Elder Cyril Miller
Retired Seventh-day Adventist Church administrator

Introduction

Scripture for Hope, 9/11 and Islam Considered

Sometimes people read the end of a book to discover how the story ends. God has blessed us with the opportunity to acquire the same foresight through His Word. Join me in reading the final chapter of the book of Revelation to see the promises and admonitions of God as we attempt to make sense of current and end-time events.

And he showed me a pure river of water of life, clear as crystal, proceeding out of the throne of God and of the Lamb. (2) In the midst of the street of it, and on either side of the river, [was there] the tree of life, which bare twelve [manner of] fruits, [and] yielded her fruit every month: and the leaves of the tree [were] for the healing of the nations. (3) And there shall be no more curse: but the throne of God and of the Lamb shall be in it; and his servants shall serve him: (4) And they shall see his face; and his name [shall be] in their foreheads. (5) And there shall be no night there; and they need no candle, neither light of the sun; for the Lord God giveth them light: and they shall reign for ever and ever. (6) And he said unto me, These sayings [are] faithful and true: and the Lord God of the holy prophets sent his angel to show unto his servants the things which must shortly be done. (7) Behold, I come quickly: blessed [is] he that keepeth the sayings of the prophecy of this book. (8) And I John saw these things, and heard [them]. And when I had heard and seen, I fell down to worship before the feet of the angel which showed me these things. (9) Then saith he unto me, See [thou do it] not: for I am thy fellow servant, and of thy brethren the prophets, and of them which keep the sayings of this book: worship God. (10) And he saith unto me, Seal not the sayings of the prophecy of this book: for the time is at hand. (11) He that is unjust, let him be unjust still: and he which is filthy, let him be filthy still: and he that is righteous, let him be righteous still: and he that is holy, let him be holy still. (12) And, behold, I come quickly; and my reward [is] with me, to give every man according as his work shall be. (13) I am Alpha and Omega, the beginning and the end, the first and the last. (14) Blessed [are] they that do his commandments, that they may have right to the tree of life, and may enter in through the gates into the city. (15) For without [are] dogs, and sorcerers, and whoremongers, and murderers, and idolaters, and whosoever loveth and maketh a lie. (16) I Jesus have sent mine angel to testify unto you these things in the churches. I am the root and the offspring of David, [and] the bright and morning star. (17) And the Spirit and the bride say, Come. And let him that heareth say, Come. And let him that is athirst come. And whosoever will, let him take the water of life freely. (18) For I testify unto every man that heareth the words of the prophecy of this book, If any man shall add unto these things, God shall add unto him the plagues that are written in this book: (19) And if any man shall take away from the words of the book of this prophecy, God shall take away his part out of the book of life, and out of the holy city, and [from] the things which are written in this book. (20) He which testifieth these things saith, Surely I come quickly. Amen. Even so, come, Lord Jesus. (21) The grace of our Lord Jesus Christ [be] with you all. Amen (Revelation 22:1-21).

The book of Revelation makes the end-time events clear. In Revelation 22:1, we see the river of life flowing from the throne of God, conveying His promise of heaven. The promises given in the book of Revelation are "faithful and true" (Revelation 22:6).

"Behold, I come quickly," God says, "blessed [is] he that keepeth the sayings of the prophecy of this book" (Revelation 22:7). In verse 11, the judgment is completed with the unjust and righteous both retaining the characters they have developed through their lives. The rewards of the unjust and righteous are both set before Christ returns. The condition for going to heaven is clearly given: "Blessed [are] they that do his commandments, that they may have right to the tree of life, and may enter in through the gates into the city" (Revelation 22:12, 14). The righteous are also invited to partake in the water of life freely (Revelation 22:17).

Along with these promises, a solemn warning is given to anyone who adds or takes away from these prophecies. The God of heaven is very clear. If we are to be the beneficiaries of this book and add or detract anything to or from God's Word, we will have the plagues added to our sentence and our names deleted from the book of life (Revelation 22:18, 19).

Keeping this final chapter of the Bible fresh in our minds, let us now look at the events associated with the attacks of September 11, 2001, and see what insights the Bible offers into what is happening in our world. Through a careful study, focused on Revelation 8-11, we can discover how the hand of God guided in past history, to give us an understanding of how God is guiding in the events happening all around the post 9/11 world today. Let us explore how Islam is a beneficiary of a blessing promised to Ishmael, and how these "children of the East" were a blessing to Protestants in the past, and possibly to the Remnant in these last days.

Chapter 1
An Eye-Opening Tour

O n September 11, 2001, I was in Vietnam doing a video documentary on the growth of the Seventh-day Adventist Church by Adventist World Radio. Our ministry assists the work of the Vietnamese speaker for Adventist World Radio, funding efforts to print the Third Angel's Message in Vietnam. Our production team was at Dong Ha, just south of the old DMZ, preparing to tour Highway 9 to Kah Sanh. As we ate breakfast with a European tour group, the television showed the fateful images of airplanes crashing into the World Trade Center buildings. We struggled to make sense of what had occurred; the media reports were already implicating Arab extremists in the attack.

As we boarded the tour bus after breakfast, two vacationing Israeli servicemen introduced themselves to our production group. I vividly remember their comments to me: "The only way to solve the problem with the Arabs is to kill every single one of them." I was quiet and listened, still trying to make sense of what was happening. We continued traveling in Vietnam, while more and more information filtered out from the United States. By the time we were ready to return, the airplanes had resumed flying to the United States.

Returning home, I had to quickly prepare for a trip to Ukraine in November. I had agreed to accompany a friend who was scheduled to teach a prophecy seminar at the new Adventist college in Kiev. Following the seminar, I traveled into Central Asia where one of the people we supported was doing a project in Samarkand, Uzbekistan. Upon my arrival in Samarkand after flying from Kiev via Moscow via Tashkent, I was very tired. I arrived on a Thursday in time to attend a health lecture in Russian at the local church that night. The conference provided me with a full-time translator, as English speakers were not in that area of the church in Central Asia.

On my arrival in Samarkand, I was invited to tour the city's historic landmarks. I am not a tourist at heart, but as a guest in a strange land, I agreed to see a few sights on Friday before the Sabbath arrived. The next few hours were the most enlightening experience I have had since I decided to serve the Lord in earnest over twenty years ago.

The Registan-Square Mosque is one of the most famous mosques in Central Asia, and was the first stop on my tour of Samarkand. It was so large that its massive structure extended beyond the frame of my small still camera from over a block away. After several hours exploring the massive mosque complex, I was ready to end the tour. My guide, however, insisted there was still more to see. Reluctantly I agreed to continue.

Walking back to our vehicle, my guide said that our next stop was a Muslim holy site, a shrine to the prophet Daniel. My attention perked up, so I asked, "What do you mean, a shrine to the prophet Daniel?" Local history records that around the start of the fifteenth century an army from this region of the world invaded Persia and discovered the tomb of the prophet Daniel. Returning with a portion of leg bone as a relic, they erected a shrine above a spring to house the relic. It is believed this relic protects the region from harm, danger and sickness. Although Samarkand is over 1000 miles from the ancient city of Babylon, I discovered that in this area Daniel was widely regarded as a man of God (Allah), and his legend was well-known.

Entering the shrine, I saw the marble cast that is said to contain Daniel's leg bone. The shrine curator recounted the story of Daniel and explained his significance to the region. I listened carefully, recalling the story contained in the Biblical account. As we left the shrine, I asked to visit an open-air market to shoot some background video for a production I was developing. But now time was short and at first my guide resisted. However, I persisted, indicating it was essential I get the footage. Careening around street corners on our way to the market, I glimpsed a large statue of a lion with wings. I cried for the driver to stop. After filming the statue, I asked what significance this Persian image held. No one seemed to know. At this point I began to understand the esteem that the Muslim community in this part of the world held for the Biblical prophet Daniel.

As I finished filming in the market, I asked my guide for some bottled water for the coming Sabbath. A pack of half-liter bottles was secured and I returned to my room to welcome the Sabbath (Saturday). Later that evening I broke open the plastic wrapping on the water pack and began reading one of the labels on a bottle. Written in mixed Russian and English, the image on the label depicted a Mosque. The English portion of the label read:

Magic Water

The curative water of spring "Daniyor" (Daniel) is located in Samarkand, in the district of "Chashma." The spring water is well known in Central and southeastern Asia, Middle East and China from the beginning of the XV century. The origin of the spring connected with the Prophet Daniel. At the present "Doniyor-Bek" springs is known as the place of pilgrimage for the people suffering from skin, gall stones and stomach diseases, sexual potential, bareness [sic] Chemical and biological analysis of spring water correspond to all the world standards. It is recognized the ecological [sic] pure and it is recommended both for drinking and cooking.

As I reread the label several times, my mind filled with questions. I spent the rest of my stay in Samarkand making all kinds of inquiries about Islam and its relationship to the legacy of the prophet Daniel in Central Asia, but did not receive any logical answers.

In a matter of a few hours, I began to develop the outline of an evangelistic series targeting the Muslim community based on the Biblical story of Daniel. What was it about Daniel that led the Muslims in this part of the world to accept him as a holy man? Was there an opportunity here to reach hearts and minds with other Biblical truths contained in the story of Daniel? These and other questions about effectively reaching

Islam with God's end-time truth raced through my mind. I recalled the promise found in Daniel. "And he said, Go thy way, Daniel: for the words [are] closed up and sealed till the time of the end. But go thou thy way till the end [be]: for thou shalt rest, and stand in thy lot at the end of the days" (Daniel 12:9, 13). A question formed in my mind: "Has God provided a way for His message to reach the children of Abraham and Hagar through the prophet Daniel and his profoundly meaningful end-time book?"

> And the angel of the LORD said unto her, Behold, thou [art] with child, and shalt bear a son, and shalt call his name Ishmael; because the LORD has heard thy affliction. (12) And he will be a wild man; his hand [will be] against every man, and every man's hand against him; and he shall dwell in the presence of all his brethren (Genesis 16:11, 12).

The margin of the King James Version of the Bible translates Ishmael as "God will hear".[1] I may not know what Ishmael means in the fullest sense, but I do know that the Bible means what it says. Any discussion of Christianity's relationship to the Muslim community today must take into account the books of Genesis and Daniel.

If William Miller's understanding of the books of Daniel and Revelation resulted in the "Midnight Cry" (when Turkey or Islam lost its autonomy on August 11, 1840), is it possible that a clear understanding of Daniel and Revelation and its relationship to Islam today could result in the "Loud Cry"? Could it be that the correct understanding of these end-time events will spark the awakening of the world, referred to by Ellen White as the "Loud Cry"?[2] Seventh-day Adventist Christians must be reading, studying and praying for the correct understanding of these prophetic messages in the power and blood of the Messiah.

*　　　　　　*　　　　　　*

I needed to return to Tashkent, Uzbekistan, and that meant leaving Samarkand immediately after sundown in order to maintain my schedule. Six hours overland by taxi through the Central Asian night is not my preferred method of transportation. At the central bus station, we searched the rows of dilapidated vehicles, looking for a taxi that exhibited the best chance of making the trip. The United States had just launched the invasion of Afghanistan. As we drove through the night, I stared into the blackness scanning the southern horizon for flashes of light from the battles that were underway. During my tour and two extensions (twenty-seven months) in Vietnam, I had become very familiar with night-time battles. The road ahead that night held many uncertainties.

Two hours into the journey, our taxi just quit running. No amount of praying and engine work seemed to help. My translator, the Seventh-day Adventist Central Asian Conference vice president and I were stranded on a dark, cold stretch of the old Silk Highway. Standing beside the engine holding my flashlight, our only light, I thought about the thousands of years of human history witnessed by these valley walls.

I was on high alert to the slightest sound. Bandits are a very real threat in this part of the world, especially with the anticipated influx of refugees from Afghanistan. The occasional vehicle that passed never slowed as it swerved past us and plunged on into the cold Central Asian night.

After what seemed like hours, a tired, old Russian dump truck pulled around us and stopped. Following some negotiation, our taxi was tied to the truck with a short rope. Off we lurched through the cold night. Familiar with what would happen to our towed vehicle should the dump truck make a sudden stop, I was in prayer much of the night as we bounced along. I knew that our guardian angels were in charge of the slack in the rope and protected us all night. As the sun rose over the mountains of Central Asia, we pulled into the outskirts of Tashkent, thankful to the God of heaven for His care. Despite the long night's delay, we could remain on schedule for our departure to Bishkek, Kyrgyzstan. Only time would tell what further misadventures would befall us.

[1] *Strong's Exhaustive Concordance of the Bible*, Hebrew #3458
[2] Ellen G. White, *Early Writings*, pages 261, 271 and 277

Chapter 2

Silk Highways—Detained—Plan for Central Asia

The next leg of our trip began in Tashkent after a breakfast of steaming potatoes, cabbage, beets and bread. Tashkent is located in Uzbekistan along the southern Kazakhstan border. One must travel through Kazakhstan in order to get to Bishkek, Kyrgyzstan, our destination. I was scheduled to travel with a group of people headed to the Seventh-day Adventist Church's conference office in Bishkek, a journey of about five hundred miles. Traveling through the wide, frozen boulevards of Tashkent in the early morning sun, I savored the opportunity to see the city in daylight. Recalling world history classes, I thought about the Khan and his warriors sweeping out of China and across Central Asia, conquering all in their path.

As we neared the checkpoint on the Kyrgyzstan border, the traffic congestion became a half-mile traffic jam of vehicles and cargo. Our little convoy negotiated the bottleneck as we inched towards the checkpoint. The structure marking the broad border crossing resembled a medieval castle in stainless or galvanized steel. I knew better, yet I still slid my video camera onto my lap and began filming through the car window. I did not notice the uniformed Uzbek border guard appear from the crowd and observe me using my video camera. Startled by an explosion of his commands and forceful gestures, I was ordered out of the vehicle. Without needing a word translated into English, I knew I was in trouble.

Once out of the car, I was marched to a windowless room with two chairs and a desk. At first, my translator was not allowed to join me. When the guards realized I could not speak Russian, they eventually relented and ushered in my translator and also the conference vice president. I already knew what the problem was. Pictures were not permitted at border crossings and I was in serious trouble. I thought about the others who were traveling with us and regretted delaying their trip. No one knew how long I would be detained, but with five hundred miles before us, I did not want to spend another night driving on the highways of Central Asia with a shooting war going on nearby. I also realized jail was a real possibility.

Whispering, my translator urged me to erase the incriminating video footage. Fumbling with my camera, I managed to erase most of the recent film I had taken. We waited as the guard smoked a cigarette and stared at me, telling me again that I was in deep, deep trouble. Soon he stated that the commanding officer would arrive to personally assess my crime and determine what punishment I would receive. Humbly, I prayed to my Father in heaven. I had no hope for a swift or charitable resolution. I expected that both my camera and I would be detained. I felt sorry for my family and the Seventh-day Adventist Church conference for the trouble my detention would likely cause. Finally the dreaded message came, the commanding officer had arrived.

I looked up and in walked a heavy set young man in a bright green camouflage uniform. We did not make eye contact as he approached the interrogator's desk and addressed the duty officer in Russian. As they spoke, the guard's tone changed noticeably. Turning to me, the commanding officer smiled and extended his hand. In perfect English he welcomed me to Uzbekistan.

Surprised, I explained that this was my first visit, and that I was here to find ways to assist the people of Uzbekistan. As we continued visiting, he said it was not a problem taking pictures at the border. Glancing at the guards who had apprehended me, it was obvious that they were disappointed. They could see the anticipated bonus slipping away.

Motioning for me to follow, the commanding officer stepped outside to our confiscated vehicle. He told me he had just spent one year in the United States at McAllen, Texas, stationed at the Mexican border crossing as part of a military exchange program with the United States. He went on to express how much he enjoyed his time in the United States. We talked about his family, and the future of his emerging country. Finally, we bid farewell, and I again expressed how sorry I was for the trouble I caused. We had a long way to go across Central Asia, and, by God's grace, we were again on our way.

The rest of the day was uneventful. Traveling for miles over gentle rolling and treeless hills, we passed many herds of sheep and the round dwellings called yurts. After nightfall, we arrived in Chimkent, Kazakhstan. Arriving at the home of my translator, we were met by a houseful of people. Following the introductions, I was seated at the head of the table for an elaborate meal. The father of my translator was director of the city customs service. Paperwork for everything imported into the city passed through his office. After finishing our meal, we continued on our journey and arrived in Bishkek, Kyrgyzstan, shortly after midnight.

The following morning, I met with leaders of the Seventh-day Adventist Church in Kyrgyzstan. Being familiar with past projects by our ministry in Ukraine, they wanted to discuss establishing a publishing ministry in Kyrgyzstan. In the middle of our conversation, the mission president suddenly asked what I thought of Central Asia. I shared the thoughts forming in my mind regarding the opportunities presented by the cultural and religious significance of the prophet Daniel in this part of the world. Describing what I had seen in Samarkand, I outlined a vision for reaching the Muslim mind with the gospel through the story of Daniel.

A fresh approach, or a small breakthrough, in presenting the Third Angel's Message, would be a great blessing. It is estimated that up to twenty-two percent of the world population follows the teachings of Islam. With the world's attention being focused on Islam since 9/11, I stated my belief that the time was right to focus attention on this unreached mission field.

I asked the mission president if I could experiment to see if prophecy would work using the books of Daniel and Revelation in an evangelistic effort. The goal would be to highlight the importance of the prophet Daniel and his end-time prophecies as understood by the Seventh-day Adventist Church. The mission president responded with a warm invitation to visit his territory and launch this experiment.

It was then that the mission president shared an amazing story. Under Joseph Stalin, Communist Russia undertook a massive resettlement effort to dilute ethnic majorities throughout Central Asia to minimize the possibility of regional revolts against Moscow. As a result, many ethnic Germans were relocated from western Ukraine to Kyrgyzstan. After Communism fell in 1991, German Russians were offered the option of repatriation into a united Germany. The majority of German Russians accepted this offer and, as a result, the Seventh-day Adventist Church in Kyrgyzstan lost more than twenty pastors in a single year. The mission president, Pastor Rubin Ott, was the only ethnic German pastor left in the country. In the past, conference pastors baptized up to three hundred individuals each quarter, but the net gain to the Seventh-day Adventist Church is around fifty new members or so per quarter. Pastor Ott explained that growing economic disparity and ethnic political power contributes to the continued out-migration of tens of thousands of white Russian and German minorities from Central Asia. For the Seventh-day Adventist Church to continue to grow in Central Asia, it was becoming critical to reach Islam effectively with the gospel.

Pastor Ott's closing statement challenged my mind. "If we do not find a way to reach the Muslim majority in Central Asia," he said, "we will cease to be a church in Central Asia." This was a sobering thought. I was more convinced than ever that with the proper understanding of Daniel, the Muslim mind could be reached with the gospel. I was becoming convicted that the God of heaven does have a way for the Seventh-day Adventist Church to reach the estimated twenty-two percent of the world population that are Muslims.

Chapter 3
Information Search Begins, But Where?

I returned home with a deep conviction that the Muslim acceptance of the prophet Daniel I witnessed in Central Asia could facilitate a Seventh-day Adventist presentation of the Third Angel's Message. It was December, 2001. I would spend the next two months editing and producing the Vietnamese video to assist the publishing work our ministry supports in that nation. Finishing the video late January, I could now focus on a new approach to reach the Muslims in Central Asia with the Third Angel's Message.

My intention was to enlist the help of a friend to research and compile material for this project while I focused on organizing the meetings and related logistics. My friend, who has his own ministry, was more than willing to help. However, he explained that his time would be limited due to commitments. I knew his research would be excellent, since his work already focused on the book of Daniel.

In December, 2001, I arranged a trip to see a leader in the Seventh-day Adventist Church's ministry to Islam. The meeting was short and disheartening, yet very challenging. After explaining my findings and desire to experiment using Daniel, I received perfunctory encouragement and little else. This was hardly the resounding endorsement I sought. I see now that our leaders are besieged with new plans and ideas all the time. God had many more lessons for me to learn on this journey. Thoughts of the hundreds of Seventh-day Adventist missionaries preceding me brought some encouragement. Many had answered God's call to Muslim lands only to be met with decades of disappointment and discouragement.

Thinking about the challenge ahead, I recalled a dinner meeting in the home of Glenn and Elaine Fleming years earlier, when our children were attending Country Haven Academy in the State of Washington. Whenever we met, I would listen to stories of their work in Iran as Wycliffe Bible translators. I found myself in the Fleming home many times listening late into the night to stories of their work with Muslims around the globe. For some years, I had listened intently, yet did not share their passion. Coming from the Midwest, I felt little connection to Islam, generally considering Muslims to be lost souls. Despite leaving Iran during the 1979 Islamic revolution, the Flemings remained passionate about reaching the Muslim world with God's truth. Their passion for this work is contagious, and I now count myself as one of their converts to this cause. Theirs is truly a rich legacy which inspires others to bear the yoke of service to Muslims across the world. Looking back, I now see the hand of God directing me into a work that remains a great blessing every day.

God has been very kind to this poor student, who graduated from public school after dismissal from a Seventh-day Adventist boarding academy. I recently attended my high school class reunion where I met my former English teacher from public high school. As I told her about the work of our ministry focused on writing and publishing, I could see that she was speechless. I was not her star student. I was more like her meteorite. My saving grace was my mother, a former elementary teacher, who spent long evenings, year after year, making me read. By God's grace, I was able to thank my mother many times in her closing years for her persistence in making me read those many long summer evenings.

In the fall of 1996, Elaine Fleming arranged for my wife and me to dine with a leader of the Seventh-day Adventist Church's outreach efforts to the Muslim world. At that time, the church was considering installing a small publishing operation in an area of the world where there were some signs of success in reaching Muslims with the gospel. Because of our ministry's experience in the area of publishing, I hoped to be of some assistance. The meeting seemed unproductive, and I considered it a missed opportunity. But God has His timing.

However, it was at this meeting that I received a set of cassette tapes by Robert Darnell from Glenn Fleming. These tapes told the story of a group of Muslims who accepted the seventh day as the Sabbath. I listened with interest to the tapes several times. Through these tapes, I first became aware that inroads were being made in reaching the Muslim world with the gospel. As the remnant church of Bible prophecy, the Seventh-day Adventist Church must proclaim our Third Angel's Message to the twenty-two percent of the world's population that is Muslim. We had better be asking the God of heaven for His plan for reaching Islam, because thus far our plan has not met with overwhelming success. This statement in no way detracts from the years of committed service on the part of many Adventist missionaries to the Muslim world. Hearing their stories as I interviewed these retired missionaries, I have been blessed by the personal testimonies and learned much that has made our work flow much better.

On a cold Sabbath January evening five years later, the Lord reminded me of the Darnell tapes series. I thought I had lost the original audiocassettes I was given, and although I had searched for other copies, the only ones available were so degraded by being recopied, they were unintelligible. No matter how hard I searched, I could not locate the original Darnell set given to me by the Flemings. "Dear, where do you keep the old cassette tapes we no longer listen to?" I asked my wife, who knows where everything is I cannot locate. She reminded me there is an old clothes hamper in our basement; it contained almost a bushel of old tapes.

Emptying the hamper on the floor, I sorted through hundreds of tapes looking for the ones by Elder Robert Darnell. I eventually found them bound together with a rubber band. I believe it was God's timing that led me to rediscover these precious cassettes, buried all this time. Now I was searching with renewed urgency.

Placing one of the tapes in a cassette player, the audio quality was just as I recalled — perfect. Listening to the tapes again, I sensed a profound message in Elder Darnell's presentation. His experiences as a young minister in the Mid-East Union were fascinating, and his insights on communicating the gospel effectively in the Muslim world were exactly what I needed to hear.

Elder Darnell's presentation marked the first time I heard any Seventh-day Adventist discussing the trumpets and woes of Revelation 8, 9, 10 and 11 in a historical context. His lecture included a detailed discussion of the common beliefs shared between Islam and Seventh-day Adventists. This was very insightful.

Another surprise was Elder Darnell's conviction that God's promises to Abraham extended to Hagar and Abraham's son, Ishmael. This message brought me back to the book of Genesis to re-read God's blessing to Abraham. Continuing to listen, I felt impressed that here was a very special message for the Seventh-day Adventist Church in reaching the vast, unreached world of Islam.

That evening, I searched the Internet for anyone in the Loma Linda, California, area with the last name Darnell. The telephone directory listed two names. Calling the first number, I reached Elder Darnell's widow.

Expressing my joy at finding her, I asked if she knew of other audio or published text by her late husband that I could purchase to study. She said that the tapes I possessed were the only ones that dealt with their experiences in a Muslim setting. I was thrilled, however, to discover someone who had spent a significant part of her life as a missionary in the Middle East. Graciously, she accepted my request to interview her regarding their ministry to the Islamic world. Within a week I made arrangements to visit Mrs. Darnell, accompanied by her daughter-in-law, at the Seventh-day Adventist General Conference Adventist Muslim Relations office in Loma Linda, California.

Despite my excitement concerning this information unfolding on Islam, I could not neglect the evangelistic effort my wife and I had scheduled in the Philippines for early 2002. As I worked to develop this evangelism series, I imagined how I

23

would present God's message if I were preparing this series for a Muslim audience. I was challenged by the constant realization that a presentation tailored to an Islamic audience needed to be developed very differently from the standard Seventh-day Adventist evangelistic campaign. I felt weary even before our Philippine effort began. The things I had learned and experienced over the past ninety days constantly occupied my mind. I was grateful that my wife could accompany me to help with the upcoming meetings.

Our efforts in the Philippines were both a blessing and a challenge. Three months prior to our arrival, Bible workers had been traveling tirelessly across the countryside giving Bible studies, sharing God's love in many villages. When I was first invited to conduct this evangelistic series, I asked to visit a Roman Catholic region where the Seventh-day Adventist Church was afforded limited access. While our effort did not produce the large numbers of converts seen elsewhere in the Philippines, we were blessed to see over eighty people accept the Third Angel's Message in this Roman Catholic enclave.

When our meetings finished, I regretfully informed the evangelistic team we worked with that this would likely be the last series I would hold in the Philippines. These faithful soul winners had been with us in years past; the power of God attended these workers and that was the reason for our success. Explaining the opportunities for evangelism I had discovered in Central Asia, I made it clear that this was where I believed God was calling me to invest my time and energy. Back home, I began to study in earnest the history of Islam. But I had yet to fully recognize that Islam was God's forgotten blessing for His people.

Chapter 4
The Bible and Islam

In preparation for the California meeting with Mrs. Darnell, I studied everything I could find on the history of Islam. Starting with the story of Hagar and Ishmael in Genesis, I discovered some new facets to this familiar story.

In Genesis 12, God promises Abraham that he will become a great nation through his descendants. God's promises never fail. Once He says something, it is going to happen; it will be done. A second promise that God makes to Abraham in Genesis surprised me even more— "And I will bless them that bless thee, and curse him that curseth thee: and in thee shall all families of the earth be blessed" (Genesis 12:3). This verse challenged my understanding of God's relationship to the "children of the East" (Genesis 25:6). It is understood by Bible scholars that Ishmael and his half brothers from Abraham's third wife, Keturah, were the people who became the "children of the East." Could the promise of Genesis 12:2, 3, and 7 not only apply to Abraham's descendants through Sarah, but also to his descendants through Hagar? Should Islam also be considered a blessing to the whole world? For years I had assumed that the blessings promised by God to the whole earth flowed exclusively through the descendants of Abraham and Sarah. Please consider the following explanation:

> Although not mentioned directly in the Bible, there is recorded in the Bible an outline of the Arabic people as the Children of Abraham who inhabited the "eastern country". The history of the Muslim peoples, therefore, begins with the prophet Abraham and his descendants through Ishmael, his firstborn son.
>
> The descendants of Ishmael and the other sons of Abraham through Keturah, were given the eastern country and are referred to as the children or people of the east. They are the progenitors of the Arabs. Muhammad,

the prophet of Islam, traces his lineage back to Ishmael through his first born son, Nabaioth. It's in the Bible, the Torah, Genesis 25:6, 12-18, RSV. "But to the sons of his concubines Abraham gave gifts, and while he was still living he sent them away from his son Isaac, eastward to the east country." "These are the descendants of Ishmael, Abraham's son, whom Hagar the Egyptian, Sarah's maid, bore to Abraham. These are the names of the sons of Ishmael, named in the order of their birth: Nebaioth, the first-born of Ishmael; and Kedar, Adbeel, Mibsam, Mishma, Dumah, Massa, Hadad, Tema, Jetur, Naphish, and Kedemah. These are the sons of Ishmael and these are their names, by their villages and by their encampments, twelve princes according to their tribes. (These are the years of the life of Ishmael, a hundred and thirty-seven years; he breathed his last and died, and was gathered to his kindred.) They dwelt from Havilah to Shur, which is opposite Egypt in the direction of Assyria; he settled over against all his people." The areas noted here in verse 18 are located in Central and Northern Arabia.[1]

While it is true that Abraham and Sarah acted without faith in producing an heir through Hagar, the fact remains that God's promises remain constant. The question of which promises apply to Ishmael and which promises apply to Isaac is an age-old question confronting the honest seeker of truth. Most Seventh-day Adventists assume that God's promises given through Abraham do not apply to the descendants of Ishmael.

We read the promise that God makes to Abraham as he leaves Ur of the Chaldees, " . . . in thee shall all families of the earth be blessed" (Genesis 12:1-4). Another promise is given in Genesis 13:15, 17, granting the land of Canaan to Abraham. A key question is whether or not these promises apply to Abraham exclusively, or extend through history to his descendants. In the New Testament, Paul says, "And if ye [be] Christ's, then are ye Abraham's seed, and heirs according to the promise" (Galatians 3:29). According to Paul, anyone who accepts the merits of the blood of Jesus Christ is an heir according to the promises made to Abraham. For this reason, I believe that all of God's promises made to Abraham, before Isaac was born, apply to all of his heirs today, including the heirs of Ishmael and Keturah's (Abraham's third wife) children. But the promises made by God in Genesis 17:19 to Abraham apply only to the descendants through Isaac's line (the lineage of the promised Messiah). The children of Keturah received sub-blessings through Ishmael as they amalgamated with his descendants. They became known as the "children of the East," and are included in God's covenant with Abraham through the line of Ishmael (Genesis 15:17-21; 37:25-28; Judges 6:3).

> After these things the word of the LORD came unto Abram in a vision, saying, Fear not, Abram: I (am) thy shield, (and) thy exceeding great reward. (2) And Abram said, Lord GOD, what wilt thou give me, seeing I go childless, and the steward of my house (is) this Eliezer of Damascus? (3) And Abram said, Behold to me thou hast given no seed: and, lo, one born in my house is mine heir. (4) And, behold, the word of the LORD (came) unto him, saying, This shall not be thine heir; but he that shall come forth out of thine own bowels shall be thine heir. (5) And he brought him forth abroad, and said, Look now toward heaven, and tell the stars, if thou be able to number them: and he said unto him, So shall thy seed be. (6) And he believed in the LORD; and he counted it to him for righteousness (Genesis 15:1-6).

In the first verse of the above passage, God is teaching Abraham a lesson of faith. God knows the end from the beginning and He tells Abraham that all His promises will be kept according to His timing—not theirs. More importantly, the promise given to Abraham clearly states that his heir would come from his own bowels (verse 4), and his descendants would multiply like the stars of heaven (verse 5). Obviously, there are many children of Isaac, but what of the children of Ishmael? I have come to believe that God's promises in these verses apply to all of Abraham's heirs, including the children of Ishmael.

And God said unto Abraham, As for Sarai thy wife, thou shalt not call her name Sarai, but Sarah (shall) her name (be). (16) And I will bless her, and give thee a son also of her: yea, I will bless her, and she shall be (a mother) of nations: kings of people shall be of her. (17) Then Abraham fell upon his face, and laughed, and said in his heart, Shall (a child) be born unto him that is an hundred years old? and shall Sarah, that is ninety years old, bear? (18) And Abraham said unto God, O that Ishmael might live before thee! (19) And God said, Sarah thy wife shall bear thee a son indeed; and thou shalt call his name Isaac: and I will establish my covenant with him for an everlasting covenant, (and) with his seed after him (Genesis 17:15-19).

Here in these verses, God gives the everlasting covenant to Abram and changes his name to Abraham. Sarai receives the new name of Sarah and the assurance that she will indeed be the mother of the covenant. In verse 18, Abraham cries out on behalf of Ishmael who is his only son at this time. Ishmael is the son on whom he has lavished his love, the son whom he believes to be the son of promise. One can imagine the thoughts that race through his mind. It is even possible that Abraham has told Ishmael he is the child of promise. Now God is turning his world of the past thirteen years upside down and this news devastates Abraham. When we consider the plan of God in this story, we must look at Genesis 16:1-16:

Now Sarai Abram's wife bare him no children: and she had an handmaid, an Egyptian, whose name [was] Hagar. (2) And Sarai said unto Abram, Behold now, the LORD hath restrained me from bearing: I pray thee, go in unto my maid; it may be that I may obtain children by her. And Abram hearkened to the voice of Sarai. (3) And Sarai Abram's wife took Hagar her maid the Egyptian, after Abram had dwelt ten years in the land of Canaan, and gave her to her husband Abram to be his wife. (4) And he went in unto Hagar, and she conceived: and when she saw that she had conceived, her mistress was despised in her eyes. (5) And Sarai said unto Abram, My wrong [be] upon thee: I have given my maid into thy bosom; and when she saw that she had conceived, I was despised in her eyes: the LORD judge between me and thee. (6) But Abram said unto Sarai, Behold, thy maid [is] in thy hand; do to her as it pleaseth thee. And when Sarai dealt hardly with her, she fled from her face. (7) And the angel of the LORD found her by a fountain of water in the wilderness, by the fountain in the way to Shur. (8) And he said, Hagar, Sarai's maid, whence camest thou? and whither wilt thou go? And she said, I flee from the face of my mistress Sarai. (9) And the angel of the LORD said unto her, Return to thy mistress, and submit thyself under her hands. (10) And the angel of the LORD said unto her, I will multiply thy seed exceedingly, that it shall not be numbered for multitude. (11) And the angel of the LORD said unto her, Behold, thou [art] with child, and shalt bear a son, and shalt call his name Ishmael; because the LORD hath heard thy affliction. (12) And he will be a wild man; his hand [will be] against every man, and every man's hand against him; and he shall dwell in the presence of all his brethren. (13) And she called the name of the LORD that spake unto her, Thou God seest me: for she said, Have I also here looked after him that seeth me? (14) Wherefore the well was called Beerlahairoi; behold, [it is] between Kadesh and Bered. (15) And Hagar bare Abram a son: and Abram called his son's name, which Hagar bare, Ishmael. (16) And Abram [was] fourscore and six years old, when Hagar bare Ishmael to Abram.

An Allegory

In verses one through three, God's church of the day has a church committee meeting, where it is decided to solve the problem of no heir for the family. Sarah suggests that Abraham go unto her maid and see if this would produce an heir. In verse four, the committee action is instituted and when Sarah sees that her maid Hagar has conceived, trouble begins when Hagar becomes lifted up. Sarah is not happy about the situation. In verses five and six, Sarah blames Abraham for the problem the committee created. Abraham decides the best thing now is to keep peace in the home. Then he gives Sarah the authority to do what she thinks is best. Sarah is angry and treats the servant Hagar harshly for something that Hagar did not have the position or ability to refuse. Because of the harsh treatment Hagar receives from Sarah, a member of the church committee, Hagar flees the church. It is interesting to note that there are no prayers recorded in Scripture, where Abraham and Sarah prayed about the situation or the problem they created during this time. In verse seven we see, for the first time, the phrase "angel of the LORD" is used in the Bible; this phrase will be used three more times in chapter 16. In Genesis 22:11, 15, the phrase "angel of the LORD" is used when Abraham was on the mount with a knife raised above Isaac to kill him for the sacrifice that God had told him to perform. We have always believed that this was God who stopped him from the act of killing his son. The next time "angel of the LORD" is found is in Exodus 3:2. This is about the story of Moses and the burning bush. The direct context needs to be considered to understand the importance of the words "angel of the LORD."

> And the angel of the LORD appeared unto him in a flame of fire out of the midst of a bush: and he looked, and, behold, the bush burned with fire, and the bush [was] not consumed. (3) And Moses said, I will now turn aside, and see this great sight, why the bush is not burnt. (4) And when the LORD saw that he turned aside to see, God called unto him out of the midst of the bush, and said, Moses, Moses. And he said, Here [am] I. (5) And he said, Draw not nigh hither: put off thy shoes from off thy feet, for the place whereon thou standest [is] holy ground. (6) Moreover he said, I [am] the God of thy father, the God of Abraham, the God of Isaac, and the God of Jacob. And Moses hid his face; for he was afraid to look upon God (Exodus 3: 2-6).

These five verses show that the phrase "angel of the LORD" is the God of creation. The "angel of the LORD" phrase, which is recorded in Genesis 16:7, is the first time it is found in Scripture. Now that the Word has established that it is God

Himself who is speaking to Hagar, let us look at the rest of the chapter with the understanding that the Creator God is giving the directions.

God finds Hagar by a fountain of water, after she ran away, and asks her in verse eight where she came from and where she is going. Hagar gives a very heart-felt answer, "I flee from the face of my mistress Sarah." In verse nine, God makes a profound statement, He commands her to return to her mistress and submit to the committee. This submission is based on the Word of the living God and not on man-made rules. In verse ten, God or "angel of the LORD" gives a promise that reaches into eternity, "I will multiply thy seed exceedingly, that it shall not be numbered for multitude." We need to realize that what just occurred was spoken by the mouth of God. This promise comes right down to our day. If God has given this promise about a multitude, would it not be just like God to give this multitude a way to receive salvation? God is not the Author of sin. The book you are reading explains several of the many ways God has directed this to be accomplished.

In verse eleven, God tells Hagar she is expecting a child and that his name shall be called "Ishmael" meaning, "God will hear." This is the first time in Scripture God gives the name for a child. There are very few times when God has named children in the Bible; Isaac, John the Baptist and Jesus are three that come to mind. We need to think about that God-given name for this child. Verse twelve says, "he will be a wild man; his hand [will be] against every man, and every man's hand against him; and he shall dwell in the presence of all his brethren." In these two verses, two sides to the character of Ishmael and his descendents are identified. Today we see these same two sides of his character in his modern-day descendants, called Islam. There is a side called terrorists or extremists and a side that "God will hear." What side do you have a yearning to reach for the "angel of the LORD?" If your answer is none of the above, then read on.

Verse thirteen finds Hagar responding to God: "she called the name of the LORD that spake unto her, Thou God seest me: for she said, Have I also here looked after him that seeth me?" Hagar is one of the few individuals in the Bible to see God's form, and this slave girl was given that permission. It is very interesting that western Christians have never seriously considered this portion of the story of Abraham. If God felt it was important enough to come in Person and give the name for this child and let Hagar see His back, maybe we should realize God has a plan for these people's salvation. This chapter is the basis for understanding how God has used, and will use, the power of the twelve princes of the "children of the East" as found in Genesis 17:20. The church committee is still in session. The question is, what will the committee decide to do next? You and I are members of that church committee; the Chairman of the committee has spoken (Matthew 28:18-20).

*   *   *

Before my friend and I arrived in California to meet with Elder Darnell's family, I had felt challenged in my understanding of God's covenant with Abraham. What I had accepted as fact in my understanding of the covenant now appeared to be little more than unfounded tradition. Could it be that the promises of God also applied to Hagar's descendants? Yet, I was convinced that my new understanding was based on a correct and careful re-examination of Scripture. Mrs. Darnell and her daughter-in-law had very graciously cleared their schedules for this two-day visit and willingly answered all my questions. At this time in my walk, I did not know what questions to ask. I scarcely knew where to begin and wished to learn as much as possible. My most important question at that time centered on the connection between Islam and the "children of the East." Depending in what context the "children of the East" is used, it could mean a person east of Israel, descendants of Hagar, or enemies of God's chosen people. Could they all be the same thing? I also wanted to know who, and what, Allah was and more about Muhammad.

Our discussions covered the start of the Darnell's work in the Middle East, the theology of Islam and the beliefs Islam holds in common with Seventh-day Adventists. As I listened, my conviction deepened that Muhammad might be more than just a warrior chieftain from the Arabian Peninsula. I began to understand that Muhammad had more in common with Martin Luther than I realized. He was more a reformer than a pagan war lord. This line of reasoning would place me in direct opposition to most of the Christian world's understanding of Islam and its perceived role in history.

For two days my mind was like a sponge, soaking up everything the Darnells shared. It was at this meeting that I was encouraged to visit Elder Kenneth Oster, a missionary who had spent much of his life in Iran. After learning that he lived near Weimar, California, we contacted him and made arrangements to meet a few months later.

Early in my journey, I was cautioned by Glenn and Elaine Fleming that the path I was embarking on would be a lonely one. I thought about their warning now as our research continued and our small ministry's travel budget dwindled. But I needed all the information I could glean for the evangelistic meetings we wanted to conduct in Central Asia. With God's strength and direction, I pressed on.

As I studied, a question formed in my mind. Why was no one else in the Seventh-day Adventist Church asking the same questions as I was? After all, were not the descendants of Ishmael heirs of God's promise? From the Revelation Seminars I had conducted, I recalled the lesson dealing with the seven trumpets in Revelation 8 and 9. I now realized that this lesson was written from the traditional Evangelical Protestant and Roman Catholic perspective; this is a perspective that is consistent with the views of popular western culture today. Reading that lesson again, I found it would now be very offensive to a Muslim audience. Among other problems, the lesson completely ignores Islam's more than incidental contributions to the Protestant Reformation. The time prophecy of Revelation 9:5, 15 has everything to do with supporting the Reformation, the pro-Protestant position.

A few weeks later, Elder and Mrs. Oster graciously welcomed us into their home. I traveled by bus from Minnesota to meet the Osters. One of my friends picked me up at the Reno bus depot, and we met another friend from the State of Washington when we arrived at Weimar. Together, we then drove to the Oster home. I was blessed again by God as we visited with them about their experiences preaching God's word to a Muslim audience. I was especially interested in how God led these modern pioneer missionaries to choose the Muslim world as their mission field. Listening to their story, I was awed by their courage. Preaching the gospel in an Islamic country can mean daily disappointment and worse. As these missionaries labored for little discernible gain, they would have heard stories from college classmates serving in mission stations across the world who were being blessed with hundreds of baptisms. At times it may have seemed that their efforts were for naught, but first-hand experience has taught me that this is not the case. We are using their personal accounts and insights today to re-examine Islam's role in prophetic history and to develop potentially ground-breaking methods for reaching the Muslim world. Praise God!

[1] www.Bibleinfo.com

Chapter 5
The Search for More Information

Much, 2002, found the United States making dramatic progress in Afghanistan and in the war against the Taliban. But the urgency I felt was related to the profound questions confronting us as Seventh-day Adventists—how could we reach the nearly one quarter of the world's population who are Muslim? Where was the sense of urgency and resolve on the part of our people to find a breakthrough in reaching Muslim hearts and minds? These questions must be asked if we are to reach one of the largest religious groups in the world with the message of the coming Messiah. At the official meetings that I have been invited to, sponsored by the church, the attendance has ranged from around twenty-five to eighty. Many of these attendees were new to Muslim outreach. My mind is directed to the old hymn entitled "O Where Are the Reapers?" and the chorus gives us the challenge. "Where are the reapers (for Islam)? O who will come, and share in the glory of the harvest home? O who will help us to garner in the sheaves of good from the fields of sin?"

I must pause at this point in our story to highlight the heroic work of a small group of Muslims who realized that the Qur'an points to the Bible as a source of truth, and have come to understand the Third Angel's Message. Reaching their religious brothers and sisters with the message of God's love, they have achieved small breakthroughs in certain areas of the Muslim world. Their accomplishments could fill an entire mission report on Sabbath morning, but unfortunately, their work cannot be publicized. If these locations were published, it would place their lives in extreme danger from the radical elements within Islam, the "wild man" side of Ishmael's character (Genesis 16:12). Given these realities, it is amazing that anyone would risk so much to reach out and share, but the power of God changes hearts and souls to risk all. Personally, before 9/11, I accepted the conventional Christian viewpoint, the simplistic assumptions that Muslims were anti-Christian, Allah was a false god and Muhammad was never a prophet of God.

My goal of holding evangelistic meetings in Central Asia during the fall of 2002 relied heavily on the research and participation of a good friend. But I soon realized the responsibility to achieve this goal would fall primarily to me. So I immersed myself in study and research without his help. Within a very short time the God of heaven sent others to help, who have been, and remain, a great blessing in this effort.

After my visit with Elder Oster and the Darnell family, I became increasingly impressed that our church must develop new ways to present Biblical truths to a Muslim audience. Watching 3ABN (Three Angels Broadcasting Network) and observing different ministers preaching, I wondered how a Muslim audience would react to it. This was an important question to answer before launching the evangelistic series in Central Asia. Consequences from an unfavorable reception in most parts of the Islamic world could be immediate and final. By God's grace, I hoped to avoid these difficulties.

Earlier in my life, I had experience as a major owner of a heavy equipment manufacturing company and as a self-taught engineer. Although I lacked academic research experience, the business world had taught me the value of applying systematic and persistent efforts to difficult challenges. I felt convicted by the Holy Spirit to research and develop a message specifically tailored to a Muslim audience. I felt convicted that whether or not anyone else within my church was focused on this particular task, I should answer God's call to Muslim mission work. The challenge of this calling has never been far from my mind each day since.

Impressed to revisit the beliefs of our early Advent pioneers, I studied the early Millerite movement and its understanding of Islam. The last major discussion of Islam within the early Advent movement focused around the date of August 11, 1840. The rescue of the Ottoman Turks by the allied powers of Europe on this date effectively ended the autonomy of the Ottoman Empire. This event was the "Rosetta stone" of prophetic interpretation, conclusively proving William Miller's prophetic interpretations and establishing the relationship between a prophetic day and literal year in Biblical prophecy. The provable understanding of this great prophecy originated primarily with Josiah Litch and his book, *The Probability of the Second Coming of Christ about A.D. 1843.*[1] Locating Litch's book proved difficult. I finally located a few copies, but they were only available for a very high price of hundreds of dollars, so I kept searching. Visiting my daughter in Loma Linda, California, I stopped by the Heritage Room of the E.G. White Estates. Following a brief inquiry, I found myself sitting before a microfiche reader examining Josiah Litch's book. I was pleased to learn that the entire book could be printed for ten cents per page.

Now that I had a copy of Litch's book, I could start to study in earnest the Millerite understandings, which swelled into what was later called "The Midnight Cry" by the angel who spoke to Ellen G. White, in her first vision.[2] Uncovering the work of Josiah Litch convinced me that the early pioneers knew much more than we do today about the workings of Islam and the Advent movement. One of the most startling discoveries was William Miller's *"Rules of Interpretation."* In this work, he lists his methods of Biblical interpretation for us. Some examples of these are his definitions for the terms we use today in prophetic interpretation. As I was going over each word and his definition, I came to the word "Lamb," and his meaning was Messiah. He used Isaiah 16:1; John 1:29 and Revelation 5:12 as Bible texts supporting his position. The next word on Miller's list was "Lamp," and his meaning was the "Word of God or the Mahometan Bible," using Psalms 119:105 and Revelation 8:10. Miller's pioneer position was that the Mohametan Bible was a lamp. William Miller saw that there was some light in the Qur'an pointing to the God of creation, the God of the judgment, the God of the last day.[3] This find has been one of the highlights of my ongoing research. When I came across this information, it forced me to question that if

Islam had an impact at the start of our message, would it also have an impact on the end-time work called the "Loud Cry"? I knew I was onto something that very few Seventh-day Adventists knew existed. The question I was asking myself was: "If the forerunner of our church had published something like this, what else is there in our church archives that have been forgotten and is essential for the post-9/11 church?" If you are asking the same question, now is the time to start a study program of our Pioneer SDA (Seventh-day Adventist) message. We are at the very end of time and prophecy is showing us this. Everything needs to be tested these days by Isaiah 8:20 "To the law and to the testimony: if they speak not according to this word, [it is] because [there is] no light in them." The Bible is the test of past history!

[1] This book can be found on microfiche at any Ellen G. White library.
[2] See Ellen G. White, *Early Writings*, page 13, published 1882, Review and Herald.
[3] "Adventist Pioneer Library" CD, hit #21,115.

Chapter 6
Revelation 9:1 Considered

And the fifth angel sounded, and I saw a star fall from heaven unto the earth: and to him was given the key of the bottomless pit (Revelation 9:1).

After transferring Litch's book, *The Probability of the Second Coming of Christ about A.D. 1843*, from microfiche to paper, I began reading it. I wanted to find out how Litch came up with the prediction that something would happen to the Ottoman Empire on August 11, 1840. But what struck me was his position on Revelation 9:1. According to Litch, the "star" of Revelation 9:1 is Muhammad and the power of Revelation 9 represents Islam. Although surprising to some, this interpretation is actually a long established position that I was just starting to comprehend. Reformation and post-Reformation writers, Martin Luther, Edward Gibbon, John Thomas to name a few, along with Advent and Seventh-day Adventist pioneers, understood Islam to be the power of Revelation 9. Even into the mid-twentieth century, we had SDA writers, like Roy Allan Anderson, saying that Muhammad was the "star" of Revelation 9:1.[1] Our SDA education department in the mid-fifties was saying the same thing in the twelfth grade academy Bible doctrine's book.[2] Furthermore, Litch proposes that Muhammad was once a minister of God and later lost his way. By the time I read Litch's book, I had reached the same understanding. In the *Strong's Exhaustive Concordance of the Bible*, the word "heaven" in Revelation 9:1, has one of the listed meanings as the "gospel." Let us read Revelation 9:1 again, putting in these new words in the verse: "And the fifth angel sounded, and I saw '*Muhammad*' fall from '*the gospel*' unto the earth: and to him was given the key of the 'bottomless pit'." I will cover the rest of this verse later. We as Seventh-day Adventists claim to let the Bible explain itself, but are we ready to handle this explanation? We need to quickly grasp, by God's grace and power, that the world of Islam is ready for the message of the Third Angel! Are we, as a people, ready to present it to the Islamic mind?

I know that interpreting the "star" of Revelation 9:1 as representing Muhammad runs contrary to how many modern-day interpreters understand this verse. One of the most widely accepted interpretations holds that any description of a fallen star contained in Scripture must represent the devil and his removal from heaven. Revelation 12:4 states that a third part of the stars of heaven were cast to the earth. I think any serious Bible student has to admit that it is speaking of the fallen angels being cast out of heaven to earth. One point we need to understand in our search is that the angels in this verse mean beings; in this case, real angels were cast out of heaven. If the view is accurate that whenever a star falls from heaven it is Satan, how can it be justified to place the fall of Satan in a time period after the death of Jesus Christ on the cross? The time frame of the third trumpet (Revelation 8:10, 11) is the first part of the fifth century. "Attila the Hun" fits that time perfectly, according to Dr. Albert Barnes in his Bible commentary on Revelation 8. According to Barnes, the star that fell was not the devil or his angels. The star here represents a human conqueror called "Attila the Hun." Barnes was only one of many old Protestant writers who correctly understood this star that fell was not the devil.

The school of Biblical interpretation cannot be accurate in saying that whenever a star falls it must mean Satan. If that were the case, we would have Satan falling many times after Jesus ascended to heaven. We know Satan's expulsion from heaven is not a recurring event and under no circumstance could it have occurred after the creation of man in the Garden of Eden. When we study the Bible, we must remember that our positions must bear up under the test of other Bible verses, and they must fit together and not be in conflict with each other.

Revelation 9:1 concludes with this passage: " . . . and to him was **given the key** of the **bottomless pit**." What is this "key"? How is the "key" to be used, and to whom is it given, and who had the "key" to give? Revelation 20:1 offers the answer, "And I saw an angel come down from heaven, **having the key** of the **bottomless pit** and a great chain in his hand." (emphasis added) According to these two verses, the "star" of Revelation 9:1 is **given the same "key"** as was held by the angel power of Revelation 20:1. This angel power is commonly accepted as representing Jesus Christ.

Christ is the only power born among men Who overcame temptation. He alone has the authority to bind the devil with His "key." Since the "key" (authority) originates with God in heaven, it must be Christ who gives the "key" (authority) to the "star" of Revelation 9:1. This may seem startling, but consider these terms in Revelation 9:1 (given the "key") and Revelation 20:1 (having the "key") carefully and prayerfully, and I believe you will reach the same conclusion. Yes, God empowered Muhammad just as He empowered Nebuchadnezzar to do His strange work on apostate Israel. Muhammad was born in A.D. 570, and remember what happened in prophetic history that started in A.D. 538 and extended to 1798. This was the time of the 1260-year reign of papal power over the then-known civilized world.

You may still have questions on the "star" falling, so I want to offer these Biblical quotes regarding Satan's fall from heaven. Let us examine a number of verses dealing with this event:

How art thou fallen from heaven, O Lucifer, son of the morning! [How] art thou cut down to the ground, which didst weaken the nations! (13) For thou hast said in thine heart, I will ascend into heaven, I will exalt my throne above the stars of God: I will sit also upon the mount of the congregation, in the sides of the north: (14) I will ascend above the heights of the clouds; I will be like the most High (Isaiah 14:12-14).

And his tail drew the third part of the stars of heaven, and did cast them to the earth: and the dragon stood before the woman which was ready to be delivered, for to devour her child as soon as it was born (Revelation 12:4).

These two series of verses indicate that Lucifer (Satan) was cast out of heaven long before the prophecy in Revelation 9:1 occurs. Most will agree that Satan's banishment from heaven was a singular event that is not repeated multiple times. Accepting this basic premise, it becomes very difficult to identify the "star" that falls in Revelation 9:1 as Lucifer or the devil. A person's feelings may want to make it mean the devil or Satan, but we must let the Bible explain itself.

We now have Muhammad and the faith called Islam that is represented by the "star" of Revelation 9:1. Then how do they exercise the "key" (authority) granted them by God? We know that a key locks or unlocks something — in this case, the "bottomless pit." I believe that the "bottomless pit", introduced in Revelation 9:1, identifies a geographic area in and around the Arabian Peninsula. SDA theology recognized the "bottomless pit" as the Arabian Peninsula up through the mid-twentieth century. In fact, all my research has failed to locate an alternate definition of this term among the older Seventh-day Adventist views. One Seventh-day Adventist writer identified the "bottomless pit" as the so-called Empty Quarter, which is modern Saudi Arabia. Until oil was found in the Arabian Peninsula, it was just an empty quarter that to the outside world was a bottomless pit, a large impenetrable desert. Many Arab writers on the internet refer to the Arabian Peninsula as the Empty Quarter yet today.

Before I proceed, I should cover other views on the "bottomless pit." The phrase "bottomless pit" is used seven times in the Bible, and they are all in Revelation. The first three verses are Revelation 9:1, 2, and 11. I propose that these three verses all mean the Arabian Peninsula or Empty Quarter, as other writers have recognized. The next two verses show that a beast comes out of the "bottomless pit" (Revelation 11:7 and 17:8). I believe the best way to explain these two verses is to look at the last two verses where the "bottomless pit" is used. Revelation 20:1 and 3 use the phrase "bottomless pit" as a place where the devil is cast and an angel having the "key" of the "bottomless pit." There is one common denominator for all seven verses, and that is that they all refer in one way or the other to the earth. The first three verses using the "bottomless pit" in Revelation 9 refer to the Arabian Peninsula where the believers of Islam came from. The next "bottomless pit" verse is found in Revelation 11:7. Ellen White describes this time and place as the French Revolution,[3] where the beast of atheism attempted to destroy the Bible and the seven-day cycle. But where did atheism come from? It came not from heaven, but the earth. In Revelation 17:8 it says, "The beast that thou sawest was, and is not; and shall ascend out of the bottomless pit, and go into perdition . . . ." This beast referred to here is papal Rome. Again we must ask ourselves, where did the beast come from? This power came from the earth, not heaven. The last two verses for the "bottomless pit" are found in Revelation 20. "(1) And I saw an angel come down from heaven, having the key of the bottomless pit and a great chain in his hand. (3) And cast him into the bottomless pit, and shut him up, and set a seal upon him, that he should deceive the nations no more, till the thousand years should be fulfilled: and after that he must be loosed a little season." These two verses denote that Satan is bound and cast into the "bottomless pit." Seventh-day Adventists have taught that Satan is bound not with chains, but his tempting power is taken away for a thousand years. Everyone on earth is dead from the bright appearing of Jesus' second coming and the living saints, who have passed the judgment, are taken to heaven. The point each one of these "bottomless pit" verses have in common is that they had to do with the earth in some way.

Before the time of Muhammad, migrating Bedouin tribes inhabited the deserts of Arabia. Their religious beliefs centered on pagan idol worship. These people groups were the descendants of Ishmael who had departed from the true God of heaven. One of those groups that we find in Judges 6:1 is called the Midianites. Midian was one of Abraham's sons by his third wife Keturah (Genesis 25:1-4). In Judges 6:1-6, the names Midianites and "children of the East" are used interchangeably. Keep in mind that Ishmael received the same promise that Isaac had received, except for God's promise in Genesis 17:21: "But my covenant will I establish with Isaac . . ." From a Bible study, we read that the sons of Keturah, Esau and the descendants of Lot's daughters (Ammon and Moab) intermarried with the descendants of Ishmael; these comprise the primary families of the "children of the East" in the Bible. The first Bible passage that shows this amalgamation of families is found in Genesis 37:25-28. The Bible refers to the traders taking Joseph to Egypt. The Ishmaelites and the Midianites, for the first time in the Bible, are mentioned as having become amalgamated as the same people. Part of God's promise to Hagar in Genesis 16:12 states that her son was to be in the presence of his brethren. This promise certainly holds true today, based on the modern political composition of the Middle East.

As a power granted authority by God, Muhammad made a dramatic impact on the cultural and religious practices in the Middle East. Idolatry and polytheism (more than one God) were largely eliminated, along with the consumption of swine and the drinking of alcohol. With Islam came a strong emphasis on worshiping the God (Allah) of the Book. Consider, for example, the following passages from the Qur'an:

> Not all of them are alike: of the People of the book are a portion that stand (for the right); they rehearse the signs of Allah all night long and then prostrate themselves in adoration. (114) They believe in Allah and the Last Day; they enjoin what is right and forbid what is wrong; and they (hasten in emulation) in (all) good works; they are in the ranks of the righteous (Sura 3:113, 114).

> If thou wert in doubt as to what We have revealed unto thee then ask those who have been reading the Book from before thee: the Truth hath indeed come to thee from thy Lord: so be in no wise of those in doubt (Sura 10:94).[4]

As we continue our study, we need to remember that the descendants of Abraham and his third wife, Keturah, became part of the "children of the East" along with Esau and Lot's descendants. All of these are part of Revelation 9:1.

Who are the people of the Book who believe in Christ's soon return? If you are a Seventh-day Adventist, the answer is you! No other faith on the earth has a historical prophetic message specifically for the closing period of earth's history. Muhammad also used the Bible as the basis of his religious understanding. The Qur'an reflects this influence from what it calls the "Book [Bible] from before." "If thou wert in doubt as to what We have revealed unto thee then ask those who have been reading the Book from before thee: the Truth hath indeed come to thee from thy Lord: so be in no wise of those in doubt" (Sura 10:94). Islam directs its readers to look to the people who promote these teachings from the "Book". You and I have the key to reach Islam. We need to put the key of Bible truth into Islam's locked understanding and turn the key. God will open the mind by His Holy Spirit, but where are the reapers?

Notice above in Sura 10:94 the word "Book" is capitalized; it means the Holy Bible. Islam instructs its adherents to respect the people of the "Book"; faithful Seventh-day Adventists are those "people of the Book". If a seeking Muslim was visiting your home, would they see the God of the "Book" exemplified in your life and home?

You may find yourself saying that it does not appear that Islam listens to any voice in Christianity. But has Islam ever heard of the Bible understandings as given to Seventh-day Adventists? Islam will reject a Christian understanding of the Word of God, because many Christians drink, eat pork and bow down to idols. We as a people have a work to do in opening the door of salvation to the Islamic population of the world. While the Bible tells us that Muhammad was granted his authority by God, it also clearly states that we are dealing with a power that fell. Like many throughout history, Muhammad did lose his way and wandered from God's truth. As Seventh-day Adventists, our church has always relied, in part, on historical events to test and prove our understanding of Biblical prophecy. To understand how Muhammad fell

45

away from the Creator God, one should read the final chapter of James Freeman Clark's great book, *Ten Great Religions, Essay in Comparative Theology.*[5] It offers the clearest picture of Muhammad's fall from grace, documenting every detail through historical sources. I believe this book must be read by the true worker seeking the lost of Islam.

It is disappointing to see more and more Seventh-day Adventists moving away from our historical moorings of prophetic understanding. Many of our people are adrift on the sea of futurism, which cannot be supported by empirical evidence from world history, the Bible or the Spirit of Prophecy. Our God, who founded this church, has not cast it adrift. Our historical prophetic understanding has been our anchor; we should not discard it so readily without sound reasons.

In closing, let us read Revelation 9:1 again with the meanings we have gleaned from this study: "And the fifth angel sounded, and I saw a star [Muhammad] fall from heaven [the gospel] unto the earth: and to him [Muhammad] was given the key [authority] of the bottomless pit [Empty Quarter, Arabia]."

---

[1] *Unfolding the Revelation*, page 90, Pacific Press Publishing Association, 1953.

[2] *Principles of Life from the Word of God*, page 266, Pacific Press Publishing Association, 1952.

[3] Ellen G. White, *Spirit of Prophecy*, Volume Four, pages 190-194, Review and Herald, 1884.

[4] *The Meaning of The Holy Qur'an*, by Abdullah Yusuf Ali, Amana Publications, 2001, Beltsville, Maryland.

[5] J. F. Clark, *Ten Great Religions, Essay in Comparative Theology*, Houghton, Mifflin and Company of Boston and New York, 1871.

Chapter 7
What is Biblical Smoke?

And he opened the bottomless pit; and there arose a smoke out of the pit, as the smoke of a great furnace; and the sun and the air were darkened by reason of the smoke of the pit. (3) and there came out of the smoke locusts upon the earth: and unto them was given power, as the scorpions of the earth have power (Revelation 9:2, 3).

These are often misunderstood verses in Revelation 9. Many Seventh-day Adventists have adopted the Uriah Smith understanding of these verses found in *Daniel and the Revelation*.

Like the noxious and even deadly vapors which the winds, particularly from the southwest, diffuse in Arabia, Mohammedanism spread from thence its pestilential influence—arose as suddenly and spread as widely as smoke arising out of the pit, the smoke of a great furnace. Such is a suitable symbol of the religion of Mohammed, of itself, or as compared with the pure light of the gospel of Jesus. It was not, like the latter, a light from heaven, but a smoke out of the bottomless pit.[1]

This view of Islam is typical of western Christian culture in stereotyping Islam as the relentless architect of Christian persecution. It is interesting to note, however, that Muhammad was born in A.D. 570, and the bishop of Rome received his authority for the western half of the divided Roman Empire in A.D. 538. God raised up a remedy (Islam) for the apostasy that developed in the Church of Rome. Throughout our study, we will see that God has controlled this power through the period of the fifth trumpet-first woe and sixth trumpet-second woe, and I believe He still controls the same power through the seventh trumpet-third woe today.

First, let us examine the term "smoke" in its Biblical context to see if we can gain a clearer understanding of it significance. Uriah Smith identified the smoke of Revelation 9 as "deadly vapors". The word "smoke" appears in forty verses throughout Scripture. Not one of these verses associates smoke with error, false doctrine, or deadly vapor. In fact the word often denotes something quite different. Consider for example, Psalms 74:1: "O God, why hast thou cast [us] of for ever? [Why] doth thine anger smoke against the sheep o thy pasture?" Here smoke represents God's anger against sin in His people. Exodus 19:18 states, "And Mount Sinai wa altogether on a smoke, because the LORD descended upon it in fire: and the smoke thereof ascended as the smoke of a furnace, and the whole mount quaked greatly." Here smoke and fire is directly associated with God's presence.

Let's pause for a moment to consider an important question. Who gave the "key" (authority) to Islam? The answer is none other than God. If God provided the "key," it make sense that He would be in the movement and directing how the "key" was to be used, just as He lead Nebuchadnezzar to place the children of Israel in bondage for an appointed time. Now consider another instance where the word smoke appears in Scripture.

> And one cried unto another, and said, Holy, holy, holy, [is] the LORD of hosts: the whole earth [is] full of his glory. (4) And the posts of the door moved at the voice of him that cried, and the house was filled with smoke. (5) Then said I, Woe [is] me! For I am undone; because I [am] a man of unclean lips, and I dwell in the midst of a people of unclean lips: for mine eyes have seen the King, the LORD of hosts (Isaiah 6:3-5).

In these verses from Isaiah, smoke is again associated with the presence of God and holiness. Keeping the previous examples of smoke and its Biblical context in mind, let us review Revelation 9:2, 3:

> And he opened the bottomless pit; and there arose a smoke out of the pit, as the smoke of a great furnace; and

the sun and the air were darkened by reason of the smoke of the pit. (3) And there came out of the smoke locusts upon the earth: and unto them was given power, as the scorpions of the earth have power (Revelation 9:2, 3).

By God's grace, a different understanding of these verses emerges than previously thought and taught in our churches and schools. Seventh-day Adventists have always believed that God providentially directs the affairs of man. These verses reveal His leading through means that are not often understood by Seventh-day Adventists today. I propose that the "smoke" of Revelation 9:2, 3 is God's presence and signifies His displeasure with the established Christian Church in Rome—a church that has adopted un-Biblical doctrines such as idol veneration, Marianism and adoration of deceased mortals. Not only did the Christian Church in Rome adopt extra-Biblical doctrines, it also changed the day of worship to Sunday in direct opposition to the Sabbath of the true God of Abraham, and a host of other apostate views. Yes, the sun and air were darkened, but it was because of the great sins His young Roman Church was promoting as truth. A judgment out of the "bottomless pit" of the Arabian Desert is described in these verses as falling against the corrupt Church of Rome. God was in the "smoke" in the air covering the sun and afflicting His apostate people, attempting to bring them back to repentance. Almost all Seventh-day Adventists who have read Daniel and the Revelation believe that the "smoke" in Revelation 9:2, 3 represents Satan darkening the sky over the Roman Church with false doctrine from Islam. But is not the church at Rome by this time already in apostasy? Has not the wilderness experience of the 1260 years started already? The Roman Church did not represent the true believer of God; the true believer was still a Sabbathkeeper. The legacy of truth was kept alive by groups of people like the Waldenses, Albigenses, Huguenots and God's Christians of the East. Everywhere the apostles scattered, they left a trail of true believers that was attacked by the powers of darkness. It was the God of the "key" who directed the events of Revelation 9, not the devil.

Revelation 9:3 describes the locusts coming out of the earth as having been granted the power of scorpions. The power symbolized by these locusts did not possess any innate authority, but rather was granted power by a higher authority. Ultimately, it is God who grants power here on earth and determines the time and place where that authority can be exercised. Let us look at the following verses:

> And the children of Israel did evil in the sight of the LORD: and the LORD delivered them into the hand of Midian seven years. (2) And the hand of Midian prevailed against Israel: [and] because of the Midianites the children of Israel made them the dens which [are] in the mountains, and caves, and strong holds. (3) And [so] it was, when Israel had sown, that the Midianites came up, and the Amalekites, and the children of the east, even they came up against them; (4) And they encamped against them, and destroyed the increase of the earth, till thou come unto Gaza, and left no sustenance for Israel, neither sheep, nor ox, nor ass. (5) For they came up with their cattle and their tents, and they came as grasshoppers for multitude; [for] both they and their camels were without number: and they entered into the land to destroy it. (6) And Israel was greatly impoverished because of the Midianites; and the children of Israel cried unto the LORD (Judges 6:1-6).

Judges 6:5 uses the term "grasshoppers" to describe the multitudes of Midianites, or the "children of the East," faced by Gideon. Revelation 9 uses the term "locusts" to describe the power that arises out of the Arabian Peninsula. In both cases the powers characterized by these closely related insects are descendants of Hagar. When you read Judges 6:1-6, you need to ask this question: Was God behind the power of the Midianites and the "children of the East"? Yes, He was, because the Bible tells us directly in Judges 6:1: "And the children of Israel did evil in the sight of the LORD: and the LORD delivered them into the hand of Midian seven years." The scorpion power granted to the followers of Muhammad who swarmed out of the Arabian Peninsula also seems consistent with a prophecy given to Hagar in Genesis 16:10-12, forecasting a wild aspect of Ishmael's character, a character that has been passed down

rough the ages. As Seventh-day Adventists, we must look
ast the sensational and extreme aspects of Islam and focus
istead on reaching hearts and minds with God's truth. God
ould have sent angels to do this work, but He is waiting to
ive you and me the blessing of sharing God's love with the
inreached people in the Muslim world. I believe that to reach
 Muslim we must have the Bible facts about how they have
een used by God in the past. If we do not use the power of
;od's word, what better power are we going to use?

The power of the "key" granted these "locusts" from the
"bottomless pit" was described as the power of scorpions. The
ting of a scorpion is painful, but seldom lethal. This principle
vas applied to the "key" (authority) granted the emerging
ower of Islam as it came from the "bottomless pit" (Empty
Quarter). Over the period of 117 years following the death of
Muhammad, Muslim conquests surged across Central Asia
nto western China, throughout North Africa and north as
ar as Poitiers, France. Consistent with Biblical prophecy, the
ting of this advance was felt as thousands died in the conflicts
elated to this expansion. This military movement of Islam
lid start the downfall of Rome, but did not deliver the death-
low. Eastern Rome did not fall until the period of the sixth
rumpet-second woe had started.

The power of scorpions granted to Islam during this
period did not include the power to kill or destroy in a prophetic sense. Keep in mind that political powers represented
in Biblical prophecy do not always correspond directly to
historical political powers or nations. The world has only
one way to understand history and that is only through the
physical eyesight of human reasoning. We, as Seventh-day
Adventists, are supposed to take the Bible as God's infallible
Word. But do we really believe that, or do we let the 6 p.m.
news drive our understanding? Later on in Revelation 9:15,
during the period of the sixth trumpet-second woe, Islam is
granted the power to kill. But for the initial expansion period
following Muhammad's death, Islam could only sting the
current political power forecast in Bible prophecy–the Roman
Catholic Church.

The spread of Islam during this period was a stinging chal
lenge to the power and authority of the new Roman Catholic
Church, which had been invested with power from the Roman
Caesar. As the Roman Empire slowly declined, the Church
of Rome emerged as the successor power forecast by Bibl
prophecy (Revelation 13:1-10). It was the dramatic advance
of Islam that ultimately contained and checked the tempora
political power of the Roman Catholic Church. Ironically, the
very shape of this containment on a map resembles a crescent
starting in southern France and northern Spain and extend
ing down through North Africa to the Middle East and on
west to China. Thus the power of Catholicism was held from
unlimited expansion during the fifth trumpet-first woe by the
swarming Muslims from the "bottomless pit," the "children
of the East" of their day.

[1] Uriah Smith, *Daniel and the Revelation*, pages 497, 498, Pacific Press Pub
lishing Association, 1944.

Chapter 8
The Seal of God

And it was commanded them that they should not hurt the grass of the earth, neither any green thing, neither any tree; but only those men which have not the seal of God in their foreheads (Revelation 9:4).

This is one of the most profound and illuminating verses in the entire book of Revelation. It is important to understand who issues and who receives the command given in this verse. Revelation 9:1 and 20:1 gives insight into who the Power is that empowers the "key"; it is none other than God. The command not to harm those with the seal of God in their forehead is issued to the power represented by the "star" that fell. (see Revelation 9:1) We know from our study of prophecy that this "star" represents Muhammad and Islam. This verse seems to indicate that those with the "seal of God in their foreheads" (those who worship God and observe His true Sabbath) are not to be harmed by the actions of the power that is granted the "key" (Revelation 9:1). For a better understanding of Islam's interaction with the early Christian church, I recommend the book entitled *Truth Triumphant*, by B. G. Wilkinson.[1] Especially important are the Introduction, chapter 17 "Aba and the Church in Persia" and chapter 18 "Timothy of Baghdad; The Church Under Mohammedan Rule." Due to the extensive spread of Christianity by the early apostles, there were numerous populations of Christians throughout the early Islamic world who still observed the Seventh-day Sabbath. In this context, the command to spare those with the "seal of God" on their foreheads suddenly makes sense (Revelation 9:4).

Uriah Smith[2] in his book, *Daniel and the Revelation*, and A. T. Jones[3] in his book, *Great Nations of Today*, both quote a profound passage from Edward Gibbon's *Decline and Fall of the Roman Empire*:

> Remember that you are always in the presence of God, on the verge of death, in the assurance of judgment, and the hope of paradise. Avoid injustice and oppression, consult with your brethren, and study to preserve the love and confidence of your troops. When you fight the battle of the Lord, acquit yourselves like men, without turning your backs; but let not your victory be stained with the blood of women and children. Destroy no palm trees nor burn any fields of corn. Cut down no fruit trees, nor do any mischief to cattle, only such as you kill to eat. When you make any covenant or article, stand to it, and be as good as your word. As you go on, you will find some religious persons who live retired in monasteries, and propose to themselves to serve God that way: let them alone, and neither kill them nor burn their monasteries. And you will find another sort of people, that belong to the synagogue of Satan, who have shaven crowns; be sure you cleave their skulls, and give them no quarter till they either turn Mohammedan or pay tribute.[4]

Revelation 9:4 states, "And it was commanded them that they should not hurt the grass of the earth, neither any green thing, neither any tree; but only those men which have not the seal of God in their foreheads," and Gibbon's account of Abu Bekr's instructions to his Muslim troops are very similar in content. (Abu Bekr succeeded Muhammad and was leader for about a year before he also died.) The implications of this correlation caused me to reevaluate my understanding of how God's hand guided human history during this turbulent period. What Revelation 9:4 reveals to the honest seeker of truth is that God was guiding the role that Islam played on the world stage and still plays today; God is still guiding. Most Christians today view history through the perspective of the Roman Catholic Church. This view generally endorses the idea that the Crusades attempted to rescue the Holy Land from heathen and ungodly Islam. It is remarkable that the majority of Evangelical Protestants, consciously or unconsciously, have come to share this perspective.

Before we leave this discussion, we must address one more point. God's people did not understand that His seal is the Seventh-day Sabbath until this truth was revealed to the founders of our faith over 150 years ago. Yet, according to Revelation 9:4, God's people received this seal hundreds of years before this truth was recognized by early Seventh-day Adventists. To resolve this apparent discrepancy, we must follow a logical line of reasoning. As Seventh-day Adventists, where do we believe God's seal will be placed on our bodies? The answer is that we are sealed in our mind, which is the control center of the human being. The frontal lobe of the brain is the area where the Holy Spirit speaks to us from God. This leads me to believe that the Sabbath seal was the mark of God throughout the entire history of the Christian church. Surprisingly, the Qur'an has strong words for people who break the Sabbath.

In Sura 2:65 Muhammad says, "And well ye knew those amongst you who transgressed in the matter of the Sabbath; we said to them: Be ye apes despised and rejected." It appears from this Qur'an verse that Mohammed understood the true Sabbath. But could have Muhammad, like so many others before and after him, fallen away from this truth and, apparently, never return to observing the day of worship ordained by God at creation? Remember that Revelation 9:1 clearly states that the "star," Muhammad (or Islam), fell and ceased being a power for righteousness in obedience to God. Despite this fall, however, Islam retained its "key" (authority) to serve as an instrument of God's judgment against the fallen Roman Church during the 1260-day prophetic time period. The fifth trumpet-first woe and sixth trumpet-second woe coincide with this period.

When noted men of the past depict periods of world history that include powerful references to the true Sabbath, we need to sit up and take notice. Our early Seventh-day Adventist writers were aware of these historical references and wrote about them with conviction. Given the special relevance

Islam holds in the public consciousness in a post-9/11 world we should follow their example.

We must never turn our backs on history. Without the context of history, the Biblical books of Daniel and Revelation are as useful as a boat without rudder or sail. Our understanding of prophecy in a historical context is what sets Seventh-day Adventists apart from any other Protestant group in the world today. History is usually considered as fact. I propose to you that Revelation 9:4 still holds unknown meaning relating to the Islamic resurgence following the attacks of September 11, 2001. I believe that a deeper understanding of Revelation 9:4 will be revealed at the appropriate time, perhaps when the church is purified by the angels of Matthew 13:49, just before the second coming of Christ.

This verse has special meaning for the faithful scattered Sabbathkeepers of the sixth millennium. I believe that in the future it will have even greater meaning for you and me as we remain faithful, by God's grace, through the coming crisis that marks Christ's soon return for His redeemed people. We must remember that the power of this passage is ultimately subservient to the will of God, and that God's plans remain as fixed as the stars in the night sky.

In the post-9/11 world, it seems natural to assume that the resurgence of the Islamic world is being motivated by the power of evil. However, the Bible and world history show something altogether different. Consider this example from an interesting article that appeared in the November, 1987 issue of the *National Geographic* magazine. The feature article in this issue is written about the conflict between Christian Europe and Suleyman the Magnificent–the great Ottoman Turkish leader who ruled during the time of Martin Luther and the Protestant Reformation. The following passage from the article covers the aftermath of the Battle of Mohacs between the Ottoman Turks and the Hungarian army:

> Next morning King Louis's body is found. As he fled, his horse slipped on a slope. Thrown, he rolled into a stream. Held down by his golden armor, he drowned,

face in the mud. "May God be merciful to him," Suley-man says, "and punish those who misled his inexperience. I came indeed in arms against him; but it was not my wish that he should be thus cut off while he had scarcely tasted the sweets of life and royalty.

[The battle of] Mohacs struck the fear of God in Europe. With Hungary gone, Austria would be next, then Germany. Earlier Luther, whose Reformation was able to take root because of the empire's distraction by the Turks, had declared that to fight against the Turks is to resist the Lord, who visits our sins with such rods.[5]

It is interesting to note the activity of Islam during the fifth and sixth trumpets — God used them to bring judgment on the apostate church of the day, as well as deliverers to the Reformers who were persecuted in calling the world back to the plain truth of the Bible. Could it be God will use Islam in the same way during the seventh trumpet-third woe for His people? Even a secular publication like *National Geographic* credits Islam with giving time for the Reformation to take root, by diverting the power of Rome to fight Islam. How do you view Islam during this time in world history? Perhaps you have never thought about it before. Let us examine the historical record.

In my research, I found many references to the kindness and fairness of Suleyman in dealing with captured prisoners. Often in a matter of weeks, they would be released to go back to their homes and farms. This was an unusual practice during this period of history. Prisoners were normally considered to be spoils of war and were treated as property, fueling an active slave trade for hundreds of years. Students of Bible history will recall that the Jewish nation was dispersed in just such a manner at the fall of Jerusalem (A.D. 70).

The comments by key figures in the Protestant Reformation regarding the role of Islam in the judgment of apostate Christianity, should cause us to reevaluate our understanding of Islam in light of its historical significance. This is especially important today, given the events that have fixed the world since the attacks of September 11, 2001. We are currently living in the time of the seventh trumpet-third woe of Revelation 10:7 and 11:14. The world is in turmoil over the role of Islam in world terrorism and political activities. The question, my friends, is whether or not you will allow God's Word as contained in the Scriptures–or the nightly news–to shape your understanding of Islam and its role in current events.

---

[1] B. G. Wilkinson, *Truth Triumpant*, Pacific Press Publishing Association, 1944.

[2] Uriah Smith, *Daniel and the Revelation*, pages 499-501, Southern Publishing Association, Madison, Tennessee, 1897.

[3] A. T. Jones, *Great Nations of Today*, page 66, Review and Herald Publishing Co., Battle Creek, Michigan, 1901.

[4] Edward Gibbon, *Decline and Fall of the Roman Empire*, Chapter LI, para. 10.

[5] *National Geographic*, November 1987, pages 580, 581.

Chapter 9

Scorpions, Locusts, Horses and Lions

And to them it was given that they should not kill them, but that they should be tormented five months: and their torment [was] as the torment of a scorpion, when he striketh a man. (6) And in those days shall men seek death, and shall not find it; and shall desire to die, and death shall flee from them. (7) And the shapes of the locusts [were] like unto horses prepared unto battle; and on their heads [were] as it were crowns like gold, and their faces [were] as the faces of men. (8) And they had hair as the hair of women, and their teeth were as [the teeth] of lions. (9) And they had breastplates, as it were breastplates of iron; and the sound of their wings [was] as the sound of chariots of many horses running to battle. (10) And they had tails like unto scorpions, and there were stings in their tails: and their power [was] to hurt men five months (Revelation 9:5-10).

These are the last verses dealing with the fifth trumpet-first woe. In Revelation 9:5, 10 are commands to the "them" power only to harm and not to kill something. I propose that the objects of these commands are prophetic symbols of political and religious powers and not of people; history records that thousands upon thousands died in the face of the Islamic expansion into and surrounding Europe.

In order to understand Revelation 9:5-10 in the context of history, we must account for this destruction of human life. The conquest of Islam was remarkable for its speed and scope. Within 117 years following Muhammad's death, the banner of the crescent flew from Southern France, down through the Iberian Peninsula, across northern Africa, through the Holy Land

and extended across Central Asia to western China. This rapid spread begins at the start of the fifth trumpet-first woe in A.D. 622 before the five months of prophetic time (150 years), described in Revelation 9:5, actually begins. (The hegira, which was the forced journey of Mohammad from Mecca to Medina, took place in A.D. 622. This began the period of the Muslim conquests.) In order to have a "king", there must be a kingdom. The five months must begin, therefore, after the Turks are organized into a kingdom under Othman, thus making the "star", or "angel of the bottomless pit" not just their leader, but (posthumously) their "king", and with that an increase in "key" (authority) power, leading up to the second woe. The first invasion by the Turks into the Eastern Roman Empire took place on July 27, 1299, thus marking the start of the five prophetic months. During this time, Eastern Rome is stung, but not killed. July 27, 1449, marks the end of the five months as well as the end of the fifth trumpet-first woe. So, the entire period of Islamic expansion begins in the period of the fifth trumpet-first woe and ends with the sixth trumpet-second woe. We need to remember that in Revelation 9:1, Islam was given the "key" to do this strange work.

Remember that the powers we are discussing are the nations of Biblical prophetic history and not necessarily precise, historical nations or states. The two concepts are very different and can cause confusion if not clarified. The Bible powers of Revelation 8:6-12 (the first four trumpets) depict the period of the fall of the pagan Roman Empire under the Caesars. During this period, political power is transferred to the bishop of Rome, and the Roman Catholic Church inherits the mantle of power and authority relinquished by the pagan Roman Caesars. "Paganism had given place to the papacy. The dragon had given to the beast 'his power, and his seat, and great authority.' Revelation 13:2. And now began the 1260 years of papal oppression foretold in the prophecies of Daniel and the Revelation. Daniel 7:25; Revelation 13:5-7."[1] The surviving political power in the western portion of the Roman Empire, the Roman Catholic Church, had by this time developed an orthodoxy in direct opposition to the true God of heaven and His law. The stage was set for the fifth trumpet-first woe to commence after A.D. 538.

Revelation 9:5 and 10 both specify the same prophetic time periods of five months (150 years of literal time). Another clue to ascertain the start and finish of these five months is in the close link they have with the 391 years and 15 days described in Revelation 9:15 and the 2300-day prophecy of Daniel 8:14. In Advent history, Josiah Litch predicted, in 1838, something was going to happen to the Turkish Empire during the month of August, 1840. In the spring of 1840, he refined his prediction to the exact date–August 11, 1840. "Allowing the first period, 150 years, to have been exactly fulfilled before Deacozes ascended the throne by permission of the Turks, and that the 391 years, fifteen days, commenced at the close of the first period, it will end on the 11th of August, 1840, when the Ottoman power in Constantinople may be expected to be broken. And this, I [Josiah Litch] believe, will be found to be the case."[2]

The basis for this startlingly accurate calculation was the correct placement in history by Edward Gibbon of the date July 27, 1449 (see Revelation 9:5, 10). The primary source for that exact date is Gibbon's, *The History of The Decline and Fall of the Roman Empire.* In today's society, we often look for a smoking gun type of proof for a supposed fact. This was not the case for Litch's study when he arrived at the August 11, 1840, time frame for an event to happen in the Ottoman Empire. His compiling of times and events came from an exhaustive search of Gibbon's work. According to Gibbon, the Islamic conquest began on July 27, 1299, with the invasion of Nicomedia (south of present-day Istanbul, Turkey) by the Islamic Othman power.[3] For the next 150 years, the growing Othman power became known as the Ottomans, and they fulfilled Biblical prophecy by repeatedly stinging the remnants of the Eastern Roman Empire. The Ottomans controlled most of this empire as the 150-year period closed. Essentially the walled city of Constantinople was all that remained of Rome's vast empire of the Caesars.

Revelation 9:6-9 provides further clues about the power that was to "hurt men five months" (Revelation 9:10). This power is described as "locusts," indicating they were without number and completely effective in their destructive force

(Revelation 9:7). In Judges 6:5, the term grasshoppers is used to show a multitude; locusts are of the same family as grasshoppers. Their battle dress is described as crowns of gold, breastplates of iron, long hair and teeth like those of a lion, symbolizing their fierce courage in battle. It is interesting to note that under the second woe, the breastplates are compared to fire. I propose that the "breastplates of iron" symbolize the tools of warfare utilized by the Ottoman Turks during the first woe—spears, swords and archery. The breastplates of fire described in the period of the second woe, would then depict the mechanical operation and use of primitive firearms in the period of the Ottoman Empire.

The force of these judgments was brought against the apostate Roman Church in direct proportion to its refusal to repent and seek forgiveness. Islamic scholars define the word *Islam* in terms such as: submission, surrender and peace. (The author is defining the word, not commenting on today's terrorist Islamic views of the word Islam.) The religious concept defined here is that complete surrender to God brings complete peace—a very beautiful and true understanding. Students of the doctrine of righteousness by faith will find this concept very familiar. These values are also consistent with the characteristics of a committed Seventh-day Adventist as described in Revelation 14:12—patience, commandment keeping and the faith of Jesus.

All of this raises an important question: How do the self-described Islamic values of submission, surrender and peace square with the portrait of Islamic extremism portrayed in the evening news? To answer this question, we need to refresh ourselves again with Genesis 16 where an Angel tells Hagar two things about her son's character. In verse 11 we learn that the name Ishmael means "God shall hear", and in verse 12, Hagar is told that Ishmael (and by extension, his descendants) will be a "wild man" dwelling among his brethren. Herein is the key to understanding the dual character of the "children of the East" and their descendants in Bible prophecy, who moved into the religion of Islam. In carrying out God's command to preach the gospel to the entire world, we must understand this duality and not focus exclusively on our negative expresions of Islam. With up to twenty-two percent of the world's population following the teachings of Islam, we cannot bypass Islam in preaching the gospel to the entire world. What will our answer in the judgment be when asked how we used our talents to reach the children of Hagar? (see Matthew 25, story of the talents) We cannot wait for others to do this work for us. God is calling the people with the talents given by God to do this work now. We also have the historical proof of how God has used the "children of the East" in the past. The correct understanding of this principal is the basis to start a work directed by the Holy Spirit with His power.

The goal of this book is to challenge you with the Biblical and historical record of how God dealt with His people whenever they fell into idol worship and apostasy. The Old Testament provides a clear record of both God's mercy and His judgment. When Israel sinned they were punished only after years of warnings by prophets bearing a message of repentance. Similarly, God waited over five hundred years to bring judgment against the apostate Christian Church in Rome that at one time was pure (Revelation 12:1).

And the rest of the men which were not killed by these plagues yet repented not of the works of their hands, that they should not worship devils, and idols of gold, and silver, and brass, and stone, and of wood: which neither can see, nor hear, nor walk: (21) Neither repented they of their murders, nor of their sorceries, nor of their fornication, nor of their thefts (Revelation 9:20, 21).

Consider what these two verses tell us. Those who do not repent are making a conscious choice. We need to keep this in mind as we continue our study of the sixth and seventh trumpets also called woes.

[1] Ellen G. White, *The Great Controversy*, page 54.
[2] *Ibid.*, pages 334, 335.
[3] Edward Gibbon, *The History of The Decline and Fall of the Roman Empire*, Book V, Chapter LXIV, page 281.

Chapter 10
Sixth Trumpet–Second Woe

And they had a king over them, (which is) the angel of the bottomless pit, whose name in the Hebrew tongue (is) Abaddon, but in the Greek tongue has (his) name Apollyon. (12) One woe is past; (and), behold, there come two woes more hereafter. (13) And the sixth angel sounded, and I heard a voice from the four horns of the golden altar which is before God, (14) Saying to the sixth angel which had the trumpet, Loose the four angels which are bound in the great river Euphrates. (15) And the four angels were loosed, which were prepared for an hour, and a day, and a month, and a year, for to slay the third part of men. (16) And the number of the army of the horsemen [were] two hundred thousand thousand: and I heard the number of them. (17) And thus I saw the horses in the vision, and them that sat on them, having breastplates of fire, and of jacinth, and brimstone: and the heads of the horses (were) as the heads of lions; and out of their mouths issued fire and smoke and brimstone. (18) By these three was the third part of men killed, by the fire, and by the smoke, and by the brimstone, which issued out of their mouths. (19) For their power is in their mouth, and in their tails: for their tails [were] like unto serpents, and had heads, and with them they do hurt. (20) And the rest of the men which were not killed by these plagues yet repented not of the works of their hands, that they should no worship devils, and idols of gold and silver, and brass, and stone, and of wood: which neither can see, nor hear, nor walk: (21) Neither repented they of their murders, nor of their sorceries, nor of their fornication, nor of their thefts (Revelation 9:11-21).

These verses cover the period of the sixth trumpet-second woe. Some writers put verse 11 in the time of the fifth trumpet-first woe. I offer for consideration that t be placed with the sixth trumpet-second woe, but it certainly has a place in the latter portion of the fifth trumpet-first woe as it transitions into the next woe. Remember this key point, the permission to kill is not granted until the time of the sixth trumpet-second woe.

Most theologians place Muhammad as the first king, or leader, of the power of the "bottomless pit" (Revelation 9:1). Following his death, for succeeding centuries, Islam lacked clear centralized leadership. History describes the ebb and flow of Saracen and Persian dynasties that existed in the Muslim world during the fifth trumpet; the Ottoman dynasty followed in the sixth trumpet. While the period between Muhammad and a unified Ottoman Empire under Suleyman the Magnificent lacked significant centralized leadership, the religion of Islam was the driving force of the movement. It was Islam that served as the central or controlling force, uniting the "children of the East" at its core. Ultimately, it is the Qur'an, and not centralized political leadership, that is the driving force of Islam throughout the Muslim world then and today. I propose that the powers in Revelation 9 associated with the trumpets and woes are best understood in terms of religious groups and cultural nations, not in terms of specific kings, popes or other political leadership. The interpretation of Revelation 9:11 is a little different as we will explain.

I propose that the king referred to in Revelation 9:11 is Muhammad. In spite of his death, the religion he founded has existed until the present time. Remember that at one time Muhammad or the "star" was not fallen, and that the subsequent fall from God's grace takes place as found in Revelation 9:1.

Another vital term to understand in Revelation 9:11 is the term "angel." Strong's Exhaustive Concordance of the Bible defines an angel as a messenger or pastor (Strong's G32. αγγελος aggelos, *ang'-el-os*; from αγγελλω aggello [probably derived from G71; compare G34; *to bring tidings*]; a *messenger*; especially an "*angel*"; by implication a *pastor*: – angel, messenger).

65

Ask any Muslim today how they view Muhammad and they will tell you that he is a messenger; the word "angel" (Revelation 9:11) reflects this in Strong's. The message of Islam continues to be transmitted throughout the world centuries after his death. In a sense, Muhammad is indeed the leader an original messenger or angel, of a religious movement whose message continues to spread across the globe. I propose that we consider the past history of Islam, what it did, how it was used Biblically and historically, to ascertain its function during these last days.

We have already established that Arabia is the "bottomless pit" of Revelation 9:2, 3. *Strong's* states that the meaning of the word Abaddon is: G3. Αβαδδων Abaddon *ab-ad-dohn'* Of Hebrew origin [H11]; a destroying angel: - Abaddon. The word Apollyon in *Strong's* states the meaning as, G623. Απολλυων Apolluon *ap-ol-loo'-ohn;* Active participle of G622; a *destroyer* (that is, Satan)-[added by Strong's]; - Apollyon. With these definitions in mind, let us re-read Revelation 9:11, adding the definitions we have learned shown below in brackets. This is what this verse is really saying to us today:

> And they [Saracens or Arabians] had a king [Muhammad] over them, which is the angel [messenger] of the bottomless pit [Arabia], whose name in the Hebrew tongue (is) Abaddon [destroying angel], but in the Greek tongue hath (his) name Apollyon [destroyer].

Understood in this context, it shows that Islam is the overriding authority in all of Revelation 9. It is given this "key" (authority) by the God of heaven. The implication of this interpretation is profound, especially for those of us in the United States who remember September 11, 2001, or 9/11. Can we now see Revelation 9:11 in a clearer understanding? Revelation 9:12 says, "One woe is past; [and], behold, there come two woes more hereafter." It is very important to have a clear picture of what transpires in the first two woes, because these two woes give us insight into what will happen in the time of the third woe, which time we are in right now. From studying prophecy we know that the seventh trumpet-third woe covers the time period from October 22, 1844, to the present time, as foretold in Revelation 11:14. We have just seen the "wild man" side of Islam, but we cannot forget about the side "God shall hear" (Genesis 16:11, 12); this is our work, bringing the gospel or Injeel (four gospels, secondary meaning New Testament) to both sides of the character of Ishmael's descendants.

> And the sixth angel sounded, and I heard a voice from the four horns of the golden altar which is before God, (14) Saying to the sixth angel which had the trumpet, Loose the four angels which are bound in the great river Euphrates. (15) And the four angels were loosed, which were prepared for an hour, and a day, and a month, and a year, for to slay the third part of men. (16) And the number of the army of the horsemen [were] two hundred thousand thousand: and I heard the number of them. (17) And thus I saw the horses in the vision, and them that sat on them, having breastplates of fire, and of jacinth, and brimstone: and the heads of the horses [were] as the heads of lions; and out of their mouths issued fire and smoke and brimstone. (18) By these three was the third part of men killed, by the fire, and by the smoke, and by the brimstone, which issued out of their mouths. (19) For their power is in their mouth, and in their tails: for their tails [were] like unto serpents, and had heads, and with them they do hurt (Revelation 9:13-19).

As the sixth angel blows his trumpet, a voice is heard in heaven from the four horns of the golden altar, which is in the holy place of the heavenly sanctuary before God. This command is also issued directly from the Power of the holy place in the heavenly sanctuary–Jesus Christ. It is given directly to the four angels of the great river Euphrates. As we have learned, angels represent messengers in Biblical prophecy. The four messengers have characteristics consistent with Islam. They receive the same power as granted to the fifth trumpet in Revelation 9:5, but now they have the added power to kill. Understanding the prophetic time-frame in which the four angels or messengers operate, we can determine their exact place in history.

"And the four angels were loosed, which were prepared for an **hour**, and a **day**, and a **month**, and a **year** (emphasis added by author), for to slay the third part of men" (Revelation 9:15). One hour in prophecy equals one twenty-fourth of a prophetic day, or fifteen literal days. One day in prophecy equals one year, one month represents thirty years and one year signifies 360 literal years. Adding the hour, day, month and year of prophetic time gives us 391 years and 15 days of literal time.

Applying this time to the period of the sixth angel, places these events clearly after the fifth trumpet. Since the five months of Revelation 9:5, 10 take place at the end of the fifth trumpet, we can place the start of the sixth trumpet on the same day that the fifth trumpet ends. Soon after the period of the sixth trumpet began on July 27, 1449, John Palaeologus died. He was the next to the last leader of the Eastern Roman Empire to lead the beleaguered remnants of that once mighty power. His death left no direct heirs to the throne. Let me quote directly from Uriah Smith:

> In the year 1449, John Palaeologus, the Greek emperor, died, but left no children to inherit his throne, and Constantine, his brother, succeeded to it. But he would not venture to ascend the throne without the consent of Amurath. (Author's understanding: The Turkish sultan was wagging war on the remnants of the empire gradually tightening the control around the walled city of Constantinople.) He therefore sent ambassadors to ask his consent, and obtained it before he presumed to call himself sovereign.
>
> Let this historical fact be carefully examined in connection with the prediction given above. This was not a violent assault made on the Greeks (Author's understanding: The Greeks now controlled what was left of the Eastern Roman Empire), by which their empire was overthrown and their independence taken away, but simply a voluntary surrender of that independence into the hands of the Turks. The authority and supremacy of the Turkish power was acknowledged when Constantine virtually said, "I cannot reign unless you permit.

But although the four angels were thus loosed by the voluntary submission of the Greeks, yet another doom awaited the seat of empire. Amurath, the sultan to whom the submission of Constantine XIII was made, and by whose permission he reigned in Constantinople, soon after died, and was succeeded in the empire, 1451, by Mohammed II, who set his heart on securing Constantinople as the seat of his empire. He accordingly made preparations for besieging and taking the city. This siege commenced on the 6th of April, 1453, and ended in the capture of the city, and the death of the last of the Constantines, on the 16th day of May following. And the eastern city of the Caesars became the seat of the Ottoman Empire.[1]

The power of the sixth trumpet was granted permission to kill and that is exactly what occurred. This power to kill expressed itself literally in the form of gunpowder and that edge is what swung the battle that finally eliminated the last remnant of Eastern Rome. Muhammad II crafted massive cannons which were capable of shooting large boulders at the walls of Constantinople. The old bow and arrow, spear and catapult weapons could not compete with the new power of gunpowder, changing the tactics of warfare in the world forever.

With the death of the Constantine dynasty and the capture of Constantinople, the Ottoman Turks destroyed the remnants of the Eastern Roman Empire. The God of prophecy granted the "key" (Revelation 9:1) to the Islamic Turkish power to destroy the last stronghold of that empire. Of course, we are referring to the official political authority of the Eastern Roman Empire. Obviously, thousands upon thousands of soldiers and civilians died throughout the conflict. At this moment a nation of Bible prophecy was officially removed from the world stage and a new power emerged — the Islamic Ottoman Turks. Bound by the Euphrates, this power was now loosed for 391 years and fifteen days. But loosed to do what?

In the city of Rome, the bishop of the Roman Church had become a power in his own right. As the head of what we now know as the Roman Catholic Church, the bishop of

Rome assumed the titles of pope, papa–the holy father of all Christendom; titles without any Biblical basis. The angel of the "bottomless pit" was given permission to kill this idol worshiping power. Rome never gave any hint that it would ever change its ways; it remained firmly opposed to God's truth as found in Daniel 7:25. The following Bible verses are clear. The enemy of God's Bible truth did not repent.

> And the rest of the men which were not killed by these plagues yet repented not of the works of their hands, that they should not worship devils, and idols of gold, and silver, and brass, and stone, and of wood: which neither can see, nor hear, nor walk: (21) Neither repented they of their murders, nor of their sorceries, nor of their fornication, nor of their thefts (Revelation 9: 20, 21).

During the 391 years and 15 days of Revelation 9:15, the Holy Spirit began to lead some within the Church of Rome to question the church's teachings. Those Catholics who tried to reform their church had the full power of the devil brought against them with all the force permitted by the God of heaven. The word Protestant came from this time in church history, because some were convicted to protest against the apostasy of the Roman Catholic Church.

As the prophetic 391 years and 15 days were ending, a man by the name of William Miller started preaching a message that included the year/day understanding of Bible prophecy found in Daniel 8:14. Miller used his understanding of the year/day prophecy to predict Christ's return in the mid-nineteenth century. A minister named Josiah Litch heard Miller's prediction and began his own research using the prophetic time periods given in Revelation 9.

Just as Josiah Litch predicted, something important did occur on August 11, 1840. The Ottoman Empire, drastically weakened since the peak of its power during the period of the Protestant Reformation, submitted itself to Britain and European powers to avoid an overthrow by Egypt. The European powers exerted strong control over the declining Ottoman Empire until 1877, when the reigning sultan suspended many of the western reforms and turned his back on the former powers that had delivered them from the hand of Egypt.

Immediately following the end of the Ottoman Empire's political power on August 11, 1840, the area we know today as the nation of Turkey underwent dramatic changes. A western legal system replaced Islamic law by the young sultan. The power of the British government was felt more and more within the declining Ottoman Empire. England tried to make this Islamic country a western dominated nation, but it failed to work over the long term. Turkey borrowed western money that funded extensive infrastructure upgrades. The massive indebtedness, which by 1875 had pushed the country to the verge of being bankrupt, eventually drove the Ottoman Empire to join the side of Germany in World War I. Over half of Turkey's GNP (Gross National Product) went to service the crushing debt load. When Germany lost the war, all of her allies lost along with her. This meant the Ottoman Empire no longer possessed its territory in the Middle East and was forced into its current borders—the modern nation of Turkey. At this point in history, the old empire was broken up by the conquering powers of the war. The nations we know today in the Middle East, except for Israel, were divided up and renamed at this time. Israel was not made a nation until 1948.

Remember that we are concerned with the prevailing power of Islam, not the specific country of Turkey or the surrounding nations. At the time of the Reformation, the power of Islam happened to be concentrated in the area of the Middle East around, and including, what we know as the nation of Turkey. A key question addressed in this book focuses on who or what Islam will look like during the last trumpet and woe of Bible prophecy? Another question remains: "Who will this Islamic power be directed against?" As we ask these questions, we need to keep in mind the two sides of the character of Ishmael found in Genesis 16:11, 12, because the God of heaven still hears the cry of every true seeker; not one is forsaken or passed by.

There are two points that must be considered: The power of Islam in the seventh trumpet-third woe time frame must reflect similar attributes that the Bible revealed previously under the fifth trumpet-first woe and sixth-trumpet-second woe in Revelation 9. Then the new beast power of Revelation 13:11-18, which gradually took over from the first beast o Revelation 13:1-10 in 1798, and has continued to exist down to our present day, must reflect similar characteristics as its predecessor possessed.

The Bible is our guide in all things relating to our lives The reason we can know that God loves us so much today i because the Bible shows us His past long suffering and love fo His individual followers as well as His leaders. If God deviated from the prophetic history of the Bible, the Word would be fallible and untrustworthy. Please consider 2 Peter 1:18-21:

> And this voice which came from heaven we heard, when we were with him in the holy mount. (19) We have also a more sure word of prophecy; whereunto ye do well that ye take heed, as unto a light that shineth in a dark place, until the day dawn, and the day star arise in your hearts: (20) Knowing this first, that no prophecy of the scripture is of any private interpretation. (21) For the prophecy came not in old time by the will of man: but holy men of God spake [as they were] moved by the Holy Ghost.

[1] Uriah Smith, *Daniel and the Revelation*, pages 508, 509.

Chapter 11

Application of the Second Woe

L et us connect Revelation 9 to some specific events in world history. In Revelation 9:1 the power that was walking with God in obedience to His will ultimately falls. This same power is given the "key" (authority) from heaven. Revelation 9:2, 3 describe the "smoke" (anger) of God ascending from the "bottomless pit." The "smoke" of God's anger is directed against His fallen church headquartered in Rome. God's anger was not directed against Muhammad and his followers, even though the "star" fell in verse 1. The Roman Church had far more light to obey for which it was responsible.

In Revelation 9:4, a command is given to the power that holds the "key" not to harm those with the seal of God. Islam, despite its fallen condition, remains subservient to the will of God. To this command, I find no countermanding verse in Revelation.

Revelation 9:11 describes Islam as the Abaddon and Apollyon of God's judgment. This verse deals with a later time period sometime after the first description of a "key" being given to that power. We now hear a voice from the heavenly sanctuary commanding the power that was given the "key" to slay or kill (Revelation 9:15).

It is interesting to examine the actions of the power holding the "key" during the historical period of the sixth trumpet-second woe (July 27, 1449, to August 11, 1840), especially in relation to the emerging conflict between the Protestant Reformation and the Roman Catholic Church. As Martin Luther nailed his thesis to the Wittenberg church door on October 31, 1517, the Roman Catholic Church was experiencing a period of moral decay. It is during this period of tumult that the Protestant Reformation took root––first in Germany, then throughout much of Northern Europe. Here is how one historian describes this difficult time for the Roman Church, but it was also the dawning of the Reformation for all true seekers of truth everywhere.

What disorders and crimes were committed in these dark ages, when impunity was to be purchased by money! What had man to fear, when a small contribution towards building a church [St. Peters Cathedral in Rome] secured him from the fear of punishment in the world to come? What hope could there be of revival when all communication between God and man was cut off, and man, an alien from God, who is the spirit and the life, moved only in a round of paltry ceremonies and sensual observances, in an atmosphere of death!

The priests were the first who yielded to this corrupting influence. By desiring to exalt themselves they became abased. They had aimed at robbing God of a ray of his glory, and placing it in their own bosoms; but their attempt had proved vain, and they had only hidden there a leaven of corruption stolen from the power of evil. The history of the age swarms with scandals. In many places, the people were delighted at seeing a priest keep a mistress, that the married women might be safe from his seductions. What humiliating scenes did the house of a pastor in those days present! The wretched man supported the woman and the children she had borne him with the tithes and offerings. His conscience was troubled: he blushed in the presence of the people, before his domestics, and before God. The mother, fearing to come to want if the priest should die, made provision against it beforehand, and robbed her own house. Her honor was lost. Her children were ever a living accusation against her. Despised by all, they plunged into quarrels and debauchery. Such was the family of the priest!   . . . These were frightful scenes, by which the people knew how to profit.

The rural districts were the scene of numerous disorders. The abodes of the clergy were often dens of corruption. Corneille Adrian at Bruges, the abbot Trinkler at Cappel, imitated the manners of the East, and had their harems. Priests, consorting with dissolute characters, frequented the taverns, played at dice, and crowned their orgies with quarrels and blasphemy.

The council of Schaffhausen forbade the priests to dance in public, except at marriages, and to carry more than one kind of arms: they decreed also that all who were found in houses of ill fame should be unfrocked. In the archbishopric of Mentz, they scaled the walls by night, and created all kinds of disorder and confusion in the inns and taverns, and broke the doors and locks. In many places the priest paid the bishop a regular tax for the woman with whom he lived, and for each child he had by her. A German bishop said publicly one day, at a great entertainment, that in one year eleven thousand priests had presented themselves before him for that purpose. It is Erasmus who relates this.[1]

Illicit sexual activity was rampant throughout the church just before the Reformation took hold. What is happening in the Church of Rome today world wide? Consider this end-time quote:

In vision I saw two armies in terrible conflict. One army was led by banners bearing the world's insignia; the other was led by the blood-stained banner of Prince Emmanuel. Standard after standard was left to trail in the dust as company after company from the Lord's army joined the foe; and tribe after tribe from the ranks of the enemy united with the commandment-keeping people of God. An angel flying in the midst of heaven put the standards of Emmanuel into many hands, while a mighty general cried with a loud voice, "Come into line. Let those who are loyal to the commandments of God and the testimony of Christ, now take their position. 'Come out from among them, and be ye separate . . . and touch not the unclean thing; and I will receive you, and will be a Father unto you, and ye shall be my sons and daughters.' Let all who will, come up to the help of the Lord, to the help of the Lord against the mighty.[2]

Is the time of the end already upon us, or is a grand revival in front of us? The immorality of the Roman Catholic clergy prepared the way for the Reformation of that day; the same immorality is happening today among its clergy. God is revealing to each seeking soul that the way of salvation is not through a church. He is preparing His people, wherever they are, for His soon return. How committed is our preparation?

In Luther's day, the Roman Church rigidly resisted the changes advocated by the Reformation. In a sense, this same attitude exists today. Pope John Paul II may have asked forgiveness for the church's past sins, but has this confession led to any real changes in doctrine or action? Some people may question our belief or may ask how anyone can know if the pope's confession was sincere or not; the answer lies in Revelation 9:20 and 21. In verse 20 it says "yet repented not" and in verse 21 it goes on to say "neither repented they" of their sins.

Viewed through the lens of Biblical doctrine, it appears little has changed within the Roman Catholic Church. These verses must be considered in the context of the sixth trumpet-second woe.

The success of the Protestant Reformation is remarkable. Its impact on Europe and its very survival are both correctly credited to God's miraculous blessing. But what was the direct instrument of that blessing? Unbiased world history shows us that it was the will of God that protected the early Reformation and it was God's use of Islam that acted as His arm of protection and deliverance. God used the star that fell, and it was granted the "key" of the "bottomless pit" for that time. This "star" or power, remember, is Islam. Could it be that God will again use Hagar's descendants to accomplish a great work for the spiritual seed of Abraham and Isaac: protection and deliverance? Please consider the following historical reference:

> When a crisis arose in the affairs of the Reformation, and the kings obedient to the Roman See had united their swords to strike, and with blow so decisive that they should not need to strike a second time, the Turk, obeying One whom he knew not, would straightway

present himself on the eastern limits of Europe, and in so menacing an attitude, that the swords unsheathed against the poor Protestants had to be turned in another quarter. The Turk was the lightning-rod that drew off the tempest. Thus did Christ cover His little flock with the shield of the Moslem.

Their furious blows fell not upon the truths at which they were aimed, and which they were meant to extirpate; they fell upon themselves. Army was dashed against army; monarch fell before monarch; one terrible tempest from this quarter met another terrible tempest from the opposite quarter, and thus the intrigues and assaults of kings and statesmen became a bulwark around the principle which it was the object of these mighty ones to undermine and destroy. Now it is the arm of her great persecutor, Charles V that is raised to defend the Church, and now it is beneath the shadow of Soliman the Turk that she [Protestants] finds asylum. How visible the hand of God! How marvelous His providence![3]

While Luther retires from view in the Wartburg, let us consider what is passing in the world. All its movements revolve around the one great central movement, which is Protestantism. The moment Luther entered within the gates of the Wartburg the political sky became overcast, and dark clouds rolled up in every quarter. First Soliman, "whom thirteen battles had rendered the terror of Germany, made a sudden eruption into Europe. He gained many towns and castles, and took Belgrad, the bulwark of Hungary, situated at the confluence of the Danube and the Save. The States of the Empire, stricken with fear, hastily assembled at Nuremberg to concert measures for the defenses of Christendom, and for the arresting of the victorious march of its terrible invader. This was work enough for the princes. The execution of the emperor's edict against Luther, with which they had been charged, must lie over till they had found means of compelling Soliman and his hordes to return to their own land. Their swords were about to be unsheathed above Luther's head, when lo, some hundred thousand Turkish scimitars are unsheathed above theirs!"[4]

To complete the embroilment, the Turk was thundering at the gates of Austria, and threatening to march right into the heart of Christendom. Passing Vienna, Soliman was pouring his hordes into Hungary; he had slain Louis, the king of that country, in the terrible battle of Mohacz; and the Arch-Duke Ferdinand of Austria, leaving the Reformers at liberty to prosecute their work of upbuilding, had suddenly quitted the Diet of Spires and gone to contest on many a bloody field his claim to the now vacant throne of Hungary. On every side the sword was busy. Armies were continually on the march; cities were being besieged; Europe was a sea on whose bosom the great winds from the four quarters of the heavens were contending in all their fury.[5]

Consider for a moment these amazing passages. Any serious student of Protestant heritage needs to read the complete works of J. A. Wylie. These are just some of the many dramatic examples of how God protected His people and judged the apostate power of persecution – the Roman Catholic Church. As we examine Rome and its continued apostasy, it is important to remember that all of the early reformers arose from the ranks of the Roman Catholic clergy. The Reformation arose from within the corrupt and apostate Christian church of the day, not from communities of historical dissenters such as the Waldensians, Huguenots and Albigenses who held on to portions of God's truth.

In the book, *History of the Reformation of the Sixteenth Century*, by J. H. Merle D'Aubigne, is this insightful statement: "But God on several occasions made use of the same instrument for the deliverance of reviving Christianity that He had employed in the destruction of corrupt Christianity."[6] This writer of Reformation history understood the work of Islam. Could it be the same today?

The following statement recorded by J. A. Wylie reveals that Luther had a deep sense of Biblical understanding of the trumpets and woes in the book of Revelation. Luther identifies the power of Revelation 9:11. It is interesting to note that here is the only place in the Bible where the Hebrew word Abaddon and the Greek word Apollyon are used. These words both translate to *destroyer* or *destroying*. Read the following passage carefully:

Again darkness gathered round, and danger threatened the Protestant Church. Two terrible storms hung lowering in the skies of the world. The one darkened the East, the other was seen rising in the West. It was the Eastern tempest that would be first to burst, men thought, and the inhabitants of Germany turned their eyes in that direction, and watched with alarm and trembling the progress of the cloud that was coming towards them. The gates of Asia had opened, and had poured out the fierce Tartar hordes on a new attempt to submerge the rising Christianity and liberty of the West under a flood of Eastern barbarism. Traversing Hungary, the Ottoman host had sat down before the walls of Vienna a week before the Marburg Conference. The hills around that capital were white with their tents, and the fertile plains beneath its walls, which the hoof of Mussulman horse had never pressed till now, were trodden by their cavalry. The besiegers were opening trenches, were digging mines, and were thundering with their cannon, and already a breach had been made in the walls. A few days and Vienna must succumb to the numbers, the impetuosity, and valor of the Ottoman warriors, and a desolate and blood-besprinkled heap would alone remain to mark where it had stood. The door of Germany burst open, the conquerors would pour along the valley of the Danube, and plant the crescent amid the sacked cities and devastated provinces of the Empire. The prospect was a terrible one. A common ruin, like avalanche on brow of Alp, hung suspended above all parties and ranks in Germany, and might at any moment sweep down upon them with resistless fury. 'It is you,' said the adherents of the old creed addressing the Lutherans, 'who have brought this scourge upon us.

It is you who have unloosed these angels of evil; they come to chastise you for your heresy. You have cast off the yoke of the Pope, and now you must bear the yoke of the Turk.' '**Not so**,' said Luther, 'it **is God who has unloosed this army, whose king is Abaddon the destroyer. They have been sent to punish us for our sins, our ingratitude for the Gospel, our blasphemies, and above all, our shedding of the blood of the righteous**.'[7] (emphasis added by author)

This passage proves Luther understood that the power of Revelation 9:11 is Islam. I believe he had the correct understanding because he must have understood the verses leading up to verse 11 in Revelation 9. He also understood that the role of Islam during this period of world history was to protect the Reformation and to bring judgments on the apostate power of Rome. There are many references that could be included in this book about Islam and the protection it gave the young Reformation, but I will close this chapter with one of the most stirring passages in Wylie's writings.

All Lutherans shall be rooted out of the land; and wherever they are found, either by clergymen or laymen, they may be seized and burned.' These two decrees appeared only to inflame the courage of those whom they so terribly menaced. The heresy, over which the naked sword was now suspended, spread all the faster. Young men began to resort to Wittenberg, and returned thence in a few years to preach the Gospel in their native land. Meanwhile the king and the priests, who had bent the bow and were about to let fly the arrow, found other matters to occupy them than the execution of Lutherans. It was the Turk who suddenly stepped forward to save Protestantism in Hungary, though he was all unaware of the service which he performed. Soliman the Magnificent, setting out from Constantinople on the 23rd of April, 1526, at the head of a mighty army, which, receiving accessions as it marched onward, was swollen at last to 300,000 Turks, was coming nearer and nearer Hungary, like the 'wasting levin.' The land now shook with terror. King Louis was without money and without soldiers. The nobility were divided into factions; the priests thought only of pursuing the Protestants; and the common people, deprived of their laws and their liberty, were without spirit and without patriotism. Zapolya, the lord of seventy-two castles, and by far the most powerful grandee in the country, sat still, expecting if the king were overthrown to be called to mount the vacant throne. Meanwhile the terrible Turk was approaching, and demanding of Louis that he should pay him tribute, under the threat of planting the Crescent on all the churches of Hungary, and slaughtering him and his grandees like "fat oxen." The edict of death passed against the Protestants still remained in force, and the monks, in the face of the black tempest that was rising in the east, were stirring up the people to have the Lutherans put to death. The powerful and patriotic Count Pemflinger had received a message from the king, commanding him to put in execution his cruel edicts against the heretics, threatening him with his severest displeasure if he should refuse, and promising him great rewards if he obeyed. The count shuddered to execute these horrible commands, nor could he stand silently by and see others execute them. He set out to tell the king that if, instead of permitting his Protestant subjects to defend their country on the battlefield, he should drag them to the stake and burn them, he would bring down the wrath of Heaven upon himself and his kingdom. On the road to Buda, where the king resided, Pemflinger was met by terrible news. While the count was exerting himself to shield the Protestants, King Louis had set out to stop the advance of the powerful Soliman. On the 29th of August his little army of 27,000 met the multitudinous hordes of Turkey at Mohacz, on the Danube. Soliman's force was fifteen times greater than that of the king. Louis gave the command of his army to the Archbishop of Cologne — an ex-Franciscan monk, more familiar with the sword than the chaplet, and who had won some glory in the art of war. When the king put on his armor: on the morning of the battle he was observed to be deadly pale. All foresaw the issue. 'Here go twenty-seven thousand Hungarians,' exclaimed Bishop Perenyi, as the host defiled past him, 'into the kingdom of heaven, as martyrs for the faith.' He consoled himself with the hope that the chancellor would survive to see to their canonization by the Pope. The issue was even more terrible than the worst anticipations of it. By evening the plain of Mohacz was covered with the Hungarian dead, piled up in gory heaps. Twenty-eight princes, five hundred nobles, seven bishops, and twenty thousand warriors lay cold in death. Escaping from the scene of carnage, the king and the Papal legate sought safety in flight. Louis had to cross a black pool which lay in his course; his horse bore him through it, but in climbing the opposite bank the steed fell backward, crushing the monarch, and giving him burial in the marsh. The Papal nuncio, like the ancient seer from the mountains of Aram, was taken and slain. **Having trampled down the king and his army, the victorious Soliman held on his way into Hungary, and slaughtered 200,000 of its inhabitants. This calamity, which thrilled all Europe, brought rest to the Protestants.** Two candidates now contested the scepter of Hungary — John Zapolya, the unpatriotic grandee who saw his king march to death, but sat still in his castle, and the Archduke Ferdinand of Austria. Both caused themselves to be crowned, and hence arose a civil war, which, complicated with occasional appearances of Soliman upon the scene, occupied the two rivals for years, and left them no leisure to carry out the persecuting edicts. In the midst of these troubles Protestantism made rapid progress. Peter Perenyi, a powerful noble, embraced the Gospel, with his two sons. Many other magnates followed his example, and settled Protestant ministers upon their domains, built churches, planted schools, and sent their sons to study at Wittenberg. The greater number of the towns of Hungary embraced the Reformation.[8] (emphasis added by author)

The statement by this writer of Protestant history says that the killing of 200,000 people thrilled all of Europe and brought rest to the Protestants is remarkable in itself, but what if that happened today; how would it bode for us, the last true Protestants? One can only imagine the response to such a statement today in the world's press and media against anyone who dared write such an article. It would be reasonable to expect that the entire force of Western military power would be brought against any Islamic power responsible for such a massive attack today. The massacre of 200,000 people in Hungary that "thrilled all Europe" occurred under the second woe of Revelation 9:12-19. Does this protection by the descendants of Ishmael seem strange? While his brothers plotted to kill Joseph, it was God who used the Ishmaelites to preserve him by taking him to Egypt (Genesis 37:23-28). Today, as we live in the time of the third woe, are we prepared as Seventh-day Adventists for the difficult times we have been told are coming to the whole world? We need to prayerfully study our Bibles and the writings of E. G. White to understand how God protects His people who are faithful. But what about our calling to take the Third Angel's Message to the world; yes, it includes in excess of 1.4 billion people who follow Islam. Our God never forgets His people; His people are also the descendants of Ishmael that God still hears (Genesis 16:11). He is faithful who called us to do His work.

[1] J. H. Merle D'Aubigne, D.D., *History of The Reformation of the Sixteenth Century*, Book 1, Chapter 3, page 18.

[2] E. G. White, *Review and Herald*, November 26, 1903.

[3] J. A. Wylie, *The History of Protestantism*, Volume I, Book Nine, chapter 1, page 473.

[4] *Ibid.*, page 476.

[5] *Ibid.*, chapter 14, page 543.

[6] J. H. Merle D'Aubigne, D.D., *History of the Reformation of the Sixteenth Century*, Volume 3, Carter's Revised Edition, Book 10, page 126.

[7] Wylie, *Ibid.*, chapter 18, pages 566-577.

[8] *Ibid.*, Volume III, Book 20, chapter 1, pages 220-221.

Chapter 12

Seventh Trumpet—Third Woe
Relation to Third Angel

Three verses specifically refer to the seventh trumpet-third woe, and each verse is found in a different chapter of Revelation. The first is Revelation 8:13: "And I beheld, and heard an angel flying through the midst of heaven, saying with a loud voice, Woe, woe, woe, to the inhabiters of the earth by reason of the other voices of the trumpet of the three angels, which are yet to sound." The second verse is Revelation 10:7 which states: "But in the days of the voice of the seventh angel, when he shall begin to sound, the mystery of God should be finished, as he has declared to his servants the prophets." The third and final reference is found in Revelation 11:14: "The second woe is past; [and], behold, the third woe cometh quickly."

The book of Revelation lists seven trumpets, which represent seven distinct historical periods in earth's history. Each of these periods is marked by significant historical events involving powers of Biblical prophecy. What is startling and unique about the final three trumpets described above, is that they are also designated as woes. Considering the massive devastation witnessed by the world under the trumpets that are not designated as woes in Revelation, it is sobering to consider the devastation under the first two trumpets, or woes, and now we are in the time of the seventh trumpet-third woe. As we have presented in previous chapters, the destruction escalates as time progresses from the fifth trumpet-first woe to the sixth trumpet-second woe. I would propose that it will continue to escalate under the time of the seventh trumpet-third woe. This time will lead into the little time of trouble and the falling of the plagues.

I once attended a camp meeting and observed a large banner above the podium that declared, "Get ready, Get ready,

Get ready." Are we ready for the impact predicted under the final woe? Despite the challenge of living as God's children during this period of time, we have the hope our Father has given us through His promise that we can "overcome as he overcame" (Revelation 3:21). This means committing to God daily, moment by moment. I urge you to study the books of Daniel, Revelation, and Matthew 23-25 to see how God has provided a way of salvation for every soul who seeks it.

The sixth trumpet-second woe ended on August 11, 1840, exactly 391 years and 15 days following the conclusion of the fifth trumpet-first woe of Revelation 9:15. Between the end of the sixth trumpet-second woe and the beginning of the seventh trumpet-third woe, there is a gap of time. We know this because Revelation 11:14 states, "The second woe is past; [and], behold, the third woe cometh quickly." The fact that we are told the third woe "cometh quickly" implies there is a period of time between the two events (Revelation 11:14). This shows it was not coming right away, but it would come quickly.

In *Bible Readings for the Home Circle* of 1888, we are shown that the seventh trumpet-third woe begins on October 22, 1844. This means there is about a four-year gap between the second and third woes (sixth and seventh trumpets). We know this because in 1838, Josiah Litch correctly predicted the end of the second woe (sixth trumpet) to happen August 11, 1840. For an account of the activity this fulfillment created, I recommend the book by J. N. Loughborough, *The Great Second Advent Movement*, Chapter 7, pages 127-134. The accuracy of this prediction validated the understanding that a day in Biblical prophecy corresponds to a literal year and brought great power to the Millerite movement in northeastern North America, as well as mission stations around the world. We now call this powerful message of William Miller, the "Midnight Cry" (*Early Writings*, page 14). Friends, we have the "Loud Cry" (*Early Writings*, page 271) to look forward to if we remain faithful in the power and "the faith of Jesus." We must be on our knees praying for guidance and understanding so that we will recognize God's call.

"And when the seven thunders had uttered their voices, I was about to write: and I heard a voice from heaven saying unto me, Seal up those things which the seven thunders uttered, and write them not" (Revelation 10:4). We know that these seven thunders occurred in the period between the sixth and seventh trumpets. In the following quote we have the only complete narrative from E. G. White on the seven thunders of Revelation 10:7.

The mighty angel who instructed John was no less a personage than Jesus Christ. Setting His right foot on the sea, and His left upon the dry land, shows the part which He is acting in the closing scenes of the great controversy with Satan. This position denotes His supreme power and authority over the whole earth. The controversy has waxed stronger and more determined from age to age, and will continue to do so, to the concluding scenes when the masterly working of the powers of darkness shall reach their height. Satan, united with evil men, will deceive the whole world and the churches who receive not the love of the truth. But the mighty angel demands attention. He cries with a loud voice. He is to show the power and authority of His voice to those who have united with Satan to oppose the truth. After these seven thunders uttered their voices, the injunction comes to John as to Daniel in regard to the little book: 'Seal up those things which the seven thunders uttered' (Revelation 10:4). These relate to future events which will be disclosed in their order. Daniel shall stand in his lot at the end of the days. John sees the little book unsealed. Then Daniel's prophecies have their proper place in the first, second, and third angels' messages to be given to the world. The unsealing of the little book was the message in relation to time.

The books of Daniel and the Revelation are one. One is a prophecy, the other a revelation; one a book sealed, the other a book opened. John heard the mysteries which the thunders uttered, but he was commanded not to write [page 100] them. The special light given to John which was expressed in the seven thunders was a delineation of events which would transpire under the first and second angels' messages. It was not best for the people to know these things, for their faith must necessarily be tested. In the order of God, most wonderful and advanced truths would be proclaimed. The first and second angels' messages had done their specific work. This is represented by the angel standing with one foot on the sea, proclaiming with a most solemn oath that time should be no longer.

This time which the angel declares with a solemn oath, is not the end of this world's history, neither of probationary time, but of prophetic time, which should precede the advent of our Lord. That is, the people will not have another message upon definite time. After this period of time, reaching from 1842 to 1844, there can be no definite tracing of the prophetic time. The longest reckoning reaches to the autumn of 1844. The angel's position with one foot on the sea, the other on the land signifies the wide extent of the proclamation of the message. It will cross the broad waters and be proclaimed in other countries, even to all the world. The comprehension of truth, the glad reception of the message is represented in the eating of the little book. The truth in regard to the time of the advent of our Lord was a precious message to our souls.[1]

Revelation 10:7 says, "But in the days of the voice of the seventh angel, when he shall begin to sound, the mystery of God should be finished, as he hath declared to his servants the prophets." What is the mystery of God that followed the sounding of the seventh trumpet-third woe?

Early Seventh-day Adventists understood the "mystery" described in Revelation 10:7 to represent the gospel spreading across the world. This understanding arose in part from the period in which they lived. Given the constraints of travel and communication, it was difficult to imagine a swift and effective diffusion of the gospel capable of reaching the entire world. While we cannot presume to know God's methods, it is much easier to envision God's message reaching the entire world in today's age of information. We will now examine what this word "mystery" represents.

[Even] the mystery which has been hid from ages and from generations, but now is made manifest to his saints: (27) To whom God would make known what [is] the riches of the glory of this mystery among the Gentiles; which is Christ in you, the hope of glory: (28) Whom we preach, warning every man, and teaching every man in all wisdom; that we may present every man perfect in Christ Jesus: (29) Whereunto I also labor, striving according to his working, which worketh in me mightily (Colossians 1:26-29).

This passage is so clear there can be no misunderstanding. According to the Apostle Paul, the mystery is "Christ in you" (Colossians 1:27). This is what the message of righteousness by faith from Waggoner and Jones was all about. This is the essence of the doctrine of righteousness by faith. Remember we must have what Christ has done for us, as well as what He will do in us, accounted to our case in the Judgment. If we are to have the hope of being righteous, Christ must be in us each and every day by His faith working through us. How can Christ be in you and me, enabling us to keep His law? The faith stated in Revelation 14:12 is the same faith that Abraham had to wait patiently to learn, and is the same faith that Jesus had in His Father. Will you and I have this same faith in our Father in heaven; will we have the same faith to believe these prophecies of the Bible?

Today the twenty-two percent of the world's population that follow Islam lack this understanding of faith and Who to have faith in. Raised in ignorance of the real gospel, their lack of true faith is influenced, in part, by past actions of the so-called Christian church, which to a Muslim today, is Roman Catholic faith. Will we as Seventh-day Adventists, compound the sins of the past and continue to turn our backs on Islam—ignoring its overwhelming need to gain the faith in the one true God who is willing to impart His truth by the Holy Spirit. (John 16:13)

"Christ in you the hope of glory" was understood and lived by the early Advent believers. This truth came to be expressed through the Sabbath commandment and is reinforced by Ezekiel 20:12, which says, "Moreover also I gave them my

Sabbaths, to be a sign between me and them, that they might know that I [am] the LORD that sanctify them." Because the Sabbath is a sign of God's sanctifying power, it came to be understood as the Seal of God. Keeping the Sabbath itself is not an automatic seal assuring one of salvation. We must accept the merits of His blood for us and be willing to accept His mind in us, to have the will to obey Him each moment of every day. (Philippians 2:5-7)

The correct understanding of the phrase: "Let this mind be in you which was also in Christ Jesus" (Philippians 2:5) was a basic tenet of faith held by Christ's true followers in the early Advent movement, otherwise Revelation 14:12 could not be possible. By 1888, false views of the concept of righteousness by faith had entered our denomination. Gradually, a shift occurred towards a theology that emphasized the law over righteousness. This came about because of a false view of the law of God. Volumes of print in denominational and supporting ministry presses have been devoted to explaining righteousness by faith. This is what Revelation 10:7 describes, "But in the days of the voice of the seventh angel, when he shall begin to sound, the mystery of God should be finished, as he hath declared to his servants the prophets." The correct understanding of the doctrine of righteousness by faith is stated as: "Here is the patience of the saints: here [are] they that keep the commandments of God, and the faith of Jesus" (Revelation 14:12). This understanding was fully revealed in the message of 1888. This is the central theme of the Bible—how we are to reveal God's character through our lives. Time and time again, the Bible clearly shows us the failures of God's people and the path to repentance. It is no different today. The mystery of God will be finished in His people. Will it be in our lifetime? This concept is brought out in Revelation 10:7, the second verse, that is directly related to the seventh trumpet-third woe. Any end-time message that does not have the message of righteousness by faith, is not an end-time message.

---

[1] Ellen G. White, *Manuscript Releases*, Volume 1, pages 99, 100.

Chapter 13
What Will Be?

I believe the most important insight that this study has to offer centers on Islam's relationship to the seventh trumpet-third woe of Revelation 8, 9, 10, and 11. We have attempted to show in the previous chapters, from the Bible and world history, how the "children of the East" have been on call by God. They evolved into a power that is still being used as a power by God today. If Islam was the power used by God to bring judgment on the apostate Roman Church, it can also be the instrument of God's judgment against the new beast power of Revelation 13:11, coming up out of the earth. I believe that this understanding is supported by evidence from the Bible, world history, Reformational history and early Adventist understanding.

At the end of the sixth trumpet-second woe, we see the world's Islamic power losing its autonomy or authority, in part, on August 11, 1840. Now, in about one hundred sixty-six years, we see an Islamic power exercising military or terroristic power again. With the loss of Ottoman Turkish autonomy in the mid-nineteenth century, the prevailing Islamic power became a debtor nation. Turkey was called the "sick man of the East." The power of Islam appeared as if it would never be able to rise again. But what do Bible prophecies indicate will happen to Islamic power as the third woe power of Revelation? Revelation 8:13 does not make any differentiation between the woes it predicts. But in Revelation 9, we see that differentiation through the escalation of those destructive powers from the first woe to the second woe. Before the world ends, the third woe will become even more destructive in power than the first two woes. Now as we are confronted with end-time events, we will have a better understanding of the dynamics taking place. God is adding another part of the puzzle to give us a clearer view of what is going on around us. He is behind every move of these actions, just as He was in Revelation 9:1, 4 and 13.

We are addicted to oil and are now seeing firsthand how the free-world's wealth is flowing into Islamic control. This dramatic influx of wealth is empowering the "wild man" side (Genesis 16:12) of the "children of the East", known today as radical Islam.

Let us now re-examine Genesis 16:7-12. I want to share with you some additional insight I have gained through the study of this familiar story.

> And the angel of the LORD found her by a fountain of water in the wilderness, by the fountain in the way to Shur. (8) And he said, Hagar, Sarai's maid, whence camest thou? And whither wilt thou go? And she said, I flee from the face of my mistress Sarai. (9) And the angel of the LORD said unto her, Return to thy mistress, and submit thyself under her hands" (Genesis 16:7-9).

The message of the "angel of the LORD" to Hagar also applies in a figurative sense. It commands Hagar's offspring to return to the true Biblical message of salvation (Genesis 16:9). By this, I mean Islam needs to accept the message of the Three Angels of Revelation 14, just as the mother of the "children of the East" was commanded by the "angel of the LORD" to return to her mistress (the woman or church) in a spiritual sense. Could this command from the "angel of the LORD" be applied in our day in a spiritual sense to the descendants of Abraham and Hagar?

> And the angel of the LORD said unto her, I will multiply thy seed exceedingly, that it shall not be numbered for multitude. (11) And the angel of the LORD said unto her, Behold, thou art with child, and shalt bear a son, and shalt call his name Ishmael; because the LORD hath heard thy affliction (Genesis 16:10, 11).

This promise is fulfilled both through the "children of the East" in Biblical history and through the estimated twenty-two percent of the world's population that worships as Muslims today. The marginal reference in the King James Bible translates Ishmael in Genesis 16:11 as "God hears." I believe the basis of this name is found in the angel of the Lord's message to Hagar, "the LORD has heard thy affliction" (Genesis 16:11). This affliction has a literal and a corresponding figurative basis. Sarah afflicted Hagar by driving her away from Abraham's household. In a figurative sense, a woman (Sarah) represents a church in Biblical prophecy. A parallel can be drawn between Sarah's treatment of Hagar and the Christian church's treatment of Islam during the crusades.

The Seventh-day Adventist Church is the only Christian denomination with a historical prophetic message for the Muslim heart and mind that makes sense to a Muslim. Any thinking Muslim will tell you that the Seventh-day Adventist Church is the closest in belief to Islam. Seventh-day Adventists are the only worldwide denomination that keeps the Sabbath of Ishmael's father, Abraham, whom Muslims revere. We support the dietary rule of not eating pork or drinking strong drink, no idol worship and worshiping God as Jesus taught in Matthew 6:9-13. How will God's church of the end times treat the children of Hagar today? You and I are that church, it is now our responsibility to get to work and seek the lost souls of Islam.

> And he will be a wild man; his hand will be against every man, and every man's hand against him; and he shall dwell in the presence of all his brethren (Genesis 16:12).

The figurative fulfillment of Genesis 16 will be in our day, before we see the coming Messiah. The final details of the time of trouble ahead for God's people and the world will include some form of the "wild man" side of the "children of the East." Genesis 16 must be understood in its full literal and figurative sense by Seventh-day Adventists if we are to be the people who reach Islam with the message of salvation, and I believe we are that people.

> And Sarah saw the son of Hagar the Egyptian, which she had born unto Abraham, mocking. (10) Wherefore she said unto Abraham, Cast out this bondwoman and

her son: for the son of this bondwoman shall not be heir with my son, [even] with Isaac. (11) And the thing was very grievous in Abraham's sight because of his son. (12) And God said unto Abraham, Let it not be grievous in thy sight because of the lad, and because of thy bondwoman; in all that Sarah hath said unto thee, hearken unto her voice; for in Isaac shall thy seed be called. (13) And also of the son of the bondwoman will I make a nation, because he [is] thy seed. (14) And Abraham rose up early in the morning, and took bread, and a bottle of water, and gave [it] unto Hagar, putting [it] on her shoulder, and the child, and sent her away: and she departed, and wandered in the wilderness of Beersheba (Genesis 21:9-14).

For years I thought of this as one of the saddest stories in the Bible. Yet, this story contains a truth that can assist us in reaching the Islamic world with the message of salvation. Hagar and Ishmael received bread and water before they were cast out into the wilderness. In a figurative sense, Muhammad or early Islam also possessed the spiritual bread and water of God's truth before falling away (Revelation 9:1) in a spiritual sense. As Seventh-day Adventists, we have the spiritual bread and water of the Third Angel's Message to share with Islam today. Are we as a people making an effort to share this blessing with Islam, or are we hiding behind the prejudices of the power of Revelation 13:11 — the United States of America? Have we accepted the devil's deceptions by believing that this power is to be the savior of the world?

For years I had read the story of Jonah and understood it as a lesson of faith and obedience, but there is another important lesson in this story that I only recently discovered. Jonah was called by God to Nineveh, a stronghold of the "children of the East." As a Jew, he did not want to go to these descendants of Hagar, whom he considered unclean.

It is not surprising that Jonah was reluctant to carry God's message to Nineveh. Being an instrument of God's judgment, Nineveh had a history of conflict with Israel. Many times Israel's sins had been reproved by judgments meted out by the "children of the East," and now God wanted Jonah to deliver a special message of salvation to these oppressors. Certainly Jonah did not consider these descendants of Ishmael as having any part in God's promises. Ultimately, God's message of salvation was delivered to Nineveh, and the entire city repented of its sins. God is seeking today to reach the descendants of Hagar with His truth. Like Jonah, we are called to share that message. As a denomination, will we answer God's call or shrink from the challenge? Will a giant fish swallow us, if we fail to hear the call of God? Islam is a challenge, and there are "giants" before us, but as Caleb said in Numbers 13:30: "Let us go up at once, and possess it; for we are well able to overcome it." My God is able, what about your God? What are we waiting for? Let us go forward in the power and grace of our Father in heaven, which He has for each one who seeks Him.

Chapter 14
Time of the Remnant

To the Seventh-day Adventist reader of the Bible, I would urge a study of the trumpets and woes predicted in Revelation 8, 9, 10, 11. I would read what the Bible says first, then I would turn to the chapters on this subject by Uriah Smith in *Daniel and the Revelation*. I have tried to demonstrate the succession and fulfillment of the trumpets and woes through history. Let us briefly review what we have covered so far in the previous chapters before we go on to the succeeding chapters.

The first four trumpet powers were fulfilled with much bloodshed (Revelation 8:6-13). Their conclusion was marked by the collapse of the pagan Western Roman Empire. In the final verse of Revelation 8, the woes are introduced in connection with the last three trumpets. According to John the Revelator, the fifth trumpet is called a woe and directly impacts the new, great idol-worshiping Christian church of the period, a church that still exists today. That woe power was given the ability, as a scorpion, to torment, but not kill (Revelation 9:3-5, 10). With the sixth trumpet-second woe, we see a command issued to the Muslim, or Islamic power, to slay "a third part of men" (Revelation 9:15). This command is issued against the apostate church in Rome, from the four horns of the golden altar, which is before God in the heavenly sanctuary (Revelation 9:13). The purpose here is not to debate the exact meaning of the expression "a third part of men" (Revelation 9:15). It is sufficient to know that the Ottoman Turks slew over 200,000 men in a few weeks during their advance through Europe.[1] J. A. Wylie reports that this action "thrilled all of Europe" and brought peace to the persecuted Protestant church in Germany.

We have also established that the decline of the Islami
power coincides with the demise of the Ottoman Turkis
power in 1840, and that the power of Islam is being reenergize
worldwide today through its oil-driven economic expansio
and the continued rise of the power of Revelation 13:11. To
day, the support of Israel by the power of Revelation 13:1
the United States, has incited the anger of Islam around th
world. Daniel 9:24 makes it very clear that the nation of Israe
was to be cut off after four hundred ninety years, and nov
it has become a nation again with the support of the powe
of Revelation 13:11. This power is going directly against th
Bible. What does all this mean for us today? How can w
know whether the events in the Islamic world are fulfilling
role predicted in Biblical prophecy?

The Bible is filled with stories of man's failures and God'
solutions. I believe the solution to the failure of the Christia
church to reach Islam with God's message of salvation is als
contained in the Bible. By God's grace, I traveled to Centra
Asia to try an experiment to reach Muslims with a message c
the true God, based on the Biblical books of Daniel and Revela
tion. The lectures and information we developed worked ver
well and offer great promise for reaching the Muslim heart an
mind with the gospel. As Seventh-day Adventists, we mus
seek direction from God's Word and allow ourselves to b
led by the Holy Spirit. In John 16:13 is the promise, "Howbei
when he, the Spirit of truth, is come, he will guide you int
all truth: for he shall not speak of himself; but whatsoever h
shall hear, (that) shall he speak: and he will show you things t
come." This promise is for us who want to reach the twenty
two percent of the world's population who claim Muhammac
as their prophet.

As we study the way God has laid out in the trumpet an
woe prophecies, we can see an escalation of destructive powe
between the first four and the final three trumpets, called woe
This is especially true during the sixth and seventh trumpets
There are two major features of the seventh trumpet-third wo
as described in Revelation. First, the truth of righteousness b
faith is revealed to God's remnant people under the seventh

rumpet (Revelation 10:7). Second, a gap of time exists between the close of the sixth trumpet, August 11, 1840, and the beginning of the seventh trumpet, October 22, 1844. This gap of time is taken up by the seven thunders in Revelation 10:3, 4 and explained in *Manuscript Releases*, Volume 1, page 100. In our discussion, I have not covered Revelation 11:15-19. These verses have been understood by Seventh-day Adventists as occurring just before, or at, the second coming of Christ at the end of the seventh trumpet. There have been many thousands of words written on these verses as to this aspect of the seventh trumpet-third woe. I will not expend any additional time on something that has already had so much written about it. This book has attempted to show that the seventh trumpet-third woe is more than just the second coming of Jesus.

Simply stated, the first two woes were brought by God to contain and bring judgments on the apostate Christian church of the period. The apostate church perverted the truth preached by Paul and the apostles, and in the period of just a few centuries, it fell away from God and became known as Babylon. This corruption of Biblical truths resulted in idolatry, supplication to the dead and the adoption of a pagan day of worship, which is Sunday. As the children of Israel were subjected to Babylonian captivity for adopting the worship practices of heathen neighbors, likewise the Lord commanded two woes (Revelation 8:13; 9:1, 13) to fall upon the apostate Christian church headquartered in Rome.

We know from Scripture that a deadly wound (Revelation 13:3) was given to the apostate Church of Rome in 1798. Today that wound is healing rapidly. According to Revelation 17, the power of the Roman Catholic Church will ultimately be fully healed and exercise great power. Until that time comes, another nation that came up after 1798 is exercising the power lost by the Church of Rome.

The power that now rules is known as the beast of Revelation 13:11, and is also known as the false prophet of Revelation 16:13. As this nation grows, prophecy predicts that it will begin to perform acts that transform it into the false prophet of Revelation 16. Remember that this power was described as a beast from the moment it emerged from the earth. While it horns were lamb-like, its voice was like a dragon (Revelatio 13:11-18).

You may question this characterization of the Unite States, a nation synonymous with concepts of freedom an liberty. If you subscribe completely to this idyllic construc it is unlikely your heritage is connected in any way to the ex periences of African Americans in the United States. To some this country is the land of freedom and opportunity, but fo the African American, the journey continues whose ancestor were slaves. A civil war was fought for the freedom of all, bu civil rights laws were not universally passed until the 1960's The fact remains that we still have a racial divide in the Unitec States today.

According to Biblical prophecy, we are living in the perio of the seventh trumpet-third woe. It is important to remembe why Islam was granted power from God during the period o the first woe. God granted Islam power during the period o the first woe in response to the apostasy of the Roman Catho lic Church at Rome. Islam was given the "key," (authority (Revelation 9:1). During the period of the first two woes, Islar served as the instrument of God's will by bringing judgmen on the fallen Christian church for her sins (Revelation 9:20, 21 Bible prophecy teaches that Islam will be granted the powe to repeat its earlier role and bring God's judgment against th beast of Revelation 13:11. It is the United States that is nov exercising the power lost by the Church of Rome through it deadly wound. With official recognition of the Vatican b Ronald Reagan in January, 1984, America officially startec to turn its back on the Protestant principles of our Pilgrin forefathers and embraced the "scarlet woman" of Revelatio 17:1-6. It is interesting to note that the dictionaries of the 1950' define the Roman Catholic Church as the "scarlet woman". As the new beast power of Revelation 13:11 transitions int(fully rejecting our God-given Protestant heritage, Islam i granted the authority by God to commence the judgment of th seventh trumpet-third woe on us. Considered in this contex there appears to be a connection between Revelation 9:11 an(

he events of 9/11 that goes beyond the coincidence of their numerical similarity. (Please note the author does not believe in the concept of a hidden numerical Bible code and all of the things that go with that understanding.) But it is interesting to note that Abaddon and Apollyon are only found in Revelation 9:11 and refer back to the power of Revelation 9:1 as a destroying power. What was destroyed on 9/11? Our comfortable, somewhat stable American lifestyle was destroyed and we now see the crumbling of America all around us.

I know this may be a new concept, but we must grasp it quickly. We are much nearer to the close of this world's history than many imagine. The judgments have already started to come. (The plagues and judgments are two different events.) As Seventh-day Adventists, we must turn our hearts and souls to the task of reaching the Muslim world with the Third Angel's Message. The promise of the "angel of the Lord" to Hagar in Genesis 16 will be fulfilled. We have a message given to us by God. Let us share that message by His power before it is too late. But, the question for each one of us is this: What is our standing before God this day? Do you and I have the assurance that our prayers for repentance and forgiveness have been answered? Do you and I beseech the powers of heaven to give you and me victory over every besetting sin listed in our book in heaven? My brothers and sisters, we must move by the power of God to higher ground by the Comforter.

Reaching the understandings of Biblical prophecy as explained in this book, I felt strongly that they should first be presented to a Muslim audience. The messages given in the Muslim meetings were different in their emphasis than this book. The same truths were delivered to them in such a way that the Muslim wanted to know more, and they were shown the need for the Messiah, the Sin-bearer. I was blessed when the Southern Union of the Euro-Asia Division offered me that opportunity. In January, 2004, I returned to Central Asia to share this understanding of Bible prophecy with a Muslim audience. Our meetings took place in a Seventh-day Adventist cultural center in the capitol city of Bishkek, Kyrgyzstan. Advertisements for these meetings ran daily on three local television stations, and the meetings opened with standing room only. The largely Muslim crowd was so great that we extended the evangelistic experiment by a week and were blessed with more people standing during the last meeting than on the first night. After our departure, the Southern Union experienced baptisms as a result of these meetings.

My primary goal in conducting these meetings was to see if the study of prophecy would hold the interest of a Muslim audience. Our results clearly showed that the prophetic approach is still very effective. The books of Daniel and Revelation, as well as selected passages from the Qur'an which pointed back to the "Book" were used. Islam calls the Bible the "Book" many times in the Qur'an. Our message was very simple, straight forward, current and believable. Yes, the message of prophecy still reaches hearts and minds by the power of the Comforter. I chose not to use any PowerPoint presentations, only the Bible with graphic banner pictures on the wall and the Holy Spirit driving home the words of life every night. E. G. White recorded a statement that still conveys a powerful message today.

> The angel, the mighty angel from heaven, is to light-en the earth with his glory, while he cries mightily with a loud voice, "Babylon the great is fallen, is fallen" (Rev. 18:2). Oh, how I wish the church to arise and shine because the glory of the Lord has risen upon her. What can we not do in God if every human agency is doing its very utmost! "Without Me ye can do nothing" (John 15:5). We would lose faith and courage in the conflict if we were not sustained by the power of God. Every form of evil is to spring into intense activity. Evil angels unite their powers with evil men, and as they have been in constant conflict and attained an experience in the best modes of deception and battle, and have been strength-ening for centuries, they will not yield the last great final contest without a desperate struggle. All the world will be on one side or the other of the question. The battle of Armageddon will be fought, and that day must find none of us sleeping. Wide-awake we must be, as wise as

virgins having oil in our vessels with our lamps. What is this? Grace, Grace.

The power of the Holy Ghost must be upon us, and the Captain of the Lord's host will stand at the head of the angels of heaven to direct the battle. Solemn events before us are yet to transpire. Trumpet after trumpet is to be sounded, vial after vial poured out one after another upon the inhabitants of the earth.[3]

Through the years and especially now, some Seventh-day Adventists have used the above statement as a basis to justify putting the seven trumpets into a future time setting. This removes them from their prophetic moorings our pioneers understood and accepted. I believe that the "trumpet after trumpet . . . to be sounded" will be the first two trumpet woes of Revelation 9. These two trumpet woes will be repeated sometime within the period of the seventh trumpet-third woe, which began on October 22, 1844. Islam must regain its power in order to carry out its third-woe activity in our day as it did under the first and second woes. It will escalate in power during the time of the third woe in a manner similar to what it did during the first two woes. I do not believe every aspect of the fifth and sixth trumpet will be repeated to the letter within the seventh trumpet, but certainly the increase of destructive power will intensify. We must keep in mind that this power has been directed by the God of heaven in the previous trumpets.

Let us review the three verses in the Bible that mention the seventh trumpet-third woe. The first is found in Revelation 8:13, "And I beheld, and heard an angel flying through the midst of heaven, saying with a loud voice, Woe, woe, woe, to the inhabiters of the earth by reason of the other voices of the trumpet of the three angels, which are yet to sound!" The second is found in Revelation 10:7, "But in the days of the voice of the seventh [trumpet] angel, when he shall begin to sound, the mystery of God should be finished, as he hath declared to his servants the prophets." The third is found in Revelation 11:14 and 15, "The second woe is past; [and], behold, the third woe cometh quickly. (15) And the seventh angel sounded; and there were great voices in heaven, saying, The kingdoms o this world are become [the kingdoms] of our Lord, and of hi Christ; and he shall reign for ever and ever."

In these series of verses, detailed explanations are no given about the first two woes. John explained about tha power, its commands, dress and where the authority cam from in Revelation 9. John's account in Revelation 8, 10 an 11 of the seventh trumpet-third woe does not explain abou that power which the "key" gave to the angel of the "bottom less pit" for the third woe. Therefore, we need to look at th first two woes for an idea of what will happen in the thir woe. We see the power to hurt was given to the first woe and the power to kill was given to the second woe. With thi we understand an escalation of action takes place from first t second woe. I propose it will continue to intensify during th third woe, because the prophetic pattern was set in the firs two woes. That pattern found in the first two woe trumpet must be repeated in the third woe trumpet. If the third woe i to have similar prophetic DNA as the first two woes, it mus be given the same power that the "key" gave to the first tw woes in Revelation 9 in order to carry on its work during th seventh trumpet-third woe in Revelation 10 and 11.

All this being said, let us give the God of heaven latitud for more light He may choose to send to His people on thi subject. He may give us clearer understandings for trumpe reapplication at a future time, but I do not believe we are ther yet, and that time may not be in God's plan. The author is full aware of the statements from the pen of E. G. White that state history will be repeated. Rather than speculating on what wil be repeated in the future, we need to understand the histori cal application of the prophecies we have been given. In th author's view, the seventh trumpet-third woe is where we ar now with Islam rising again in power.

As we look at what is being repeated, we see that it is th increase of the "wild man" side of Islamic power. We need t keep in mind that as the "wild man" side increases in power the other side that "God hears" will increase in equal propor tion. Once the seventh trumpet-third woe started on Octobe

2, 1844, the "wild side" of the "children of the East," modern-day radical Islam, was being prepared by the God of heaven o manifest the power given to it by the Giver of the "key" Revelation 20:1). As the first two woes were directed against he apostasy of the Roman Church seated in Rome, the third voe will be directed against the new power that took Rome's place in Bible history. This is the power of Revelation 13:11. Rome lost its control of the secular governments of Europe n 1798 when Napoleon's general took the pope captive. The new beast coming up out of the ground in Revelation 13:11, 12 will exercise all the power of the first beast and he will speak as a dragon: "And I beheld another beast coming up out of the earth; and he had two horns like a lamb, and he spake as a dragon. (12) And he exerciseth all the power of the first beast before him, and causeth the earth and them which dwell therein to worship the first beast, who's deadly wound was healed."

The logic for the statement that E. G. White makes that "trumpet after trumpet is to be sounded," is true, and it remains in a historical context in the third woe time frame. For understanding prophecy in the Bible, we must go to the last place in Scripture where the meaning was clear. From there we must consider all of the stated understandings in the light of known history. God chose not to give us an exact breakdown of the destructive activity of the third woe, as He did for the destructive activity of the first and second woes. I propose that the third woe must have similar prophetic application for the second beast of Revelation 13, as the first and second woes had for the first beast. This would mean that the power given to the "key of the bottomless pit" must maintain similar prophetic application or meaning. The God of heaven has not left His people without knowledge of what will happen during the third woe; we just need to look at history for the answer.

When we covered the first two woes of Revelation 9, we read in verse 5 that they were given the power of scorpions, which can hurt, but not normally kill (remember we were talking about hurting the government of Eastern Rome), but in verse 15 they were given the power to "slay." Eastern Rome was the power they slew. As the Ottoman Turks increase in power, they weakened the papal Roman power so much during the Reformation that it lost control of the governments o Europe in 1798. I would propose for your consideration tha the beast that comes up out of the earth in Revelation 13:11 turns its power over to the beast that had the deadly wound that was healed (Revelation 13:3), because it becomes so weakened by the relentless power of the "wild man" side. From Revelation 13:11-13 we can see that the beast with lamb-like horns will force the whole world to worship the first beast o Revelation 13. I would propose for your consideration that al the time the second beast is forcing the whole world to "make an image" to the first beast and making the world to worship this first beast, the third woe continues on as the judgment o God against the beast, just as this power was used in the firs two woes by God.

In response to the question of whether this "trumpet after trumpet" will be repeated in the future, the answer is "yes." The fifth and sixth trumpets will be repeated with their "key" power being increased in intensity worldwide during the time of the seventh trumpet.

The next two chapters tell the story of our meetings in Central Asia where I went to explain Bible prophecy before a Muslim audience. The last chapter gives ideas on how to share this new information with a Muslim and how it might be done.

[1] J. A. Wylie, *The History of Protestantism*, Volume III, pages 380-383.

[2] *Webster's New World Dictionary of the American Language*, College Edition 1954, page 1302.

[3] Ellen G. White, *Manuscript Releases*, Volume 14, pages 287-289.

Chapter 15

Central Asia Evangelism Experiment

I believe the prophecies of Daniel and Revelation open the way to share the message of salvation with a Muslim audience. Some of the misunderstood spiritual issues will become clear as the Biblical prophecies unfold before them. I believe God has given us the spiritual food for this group of people, our spiritual brothers and sisters. We read in Ezekiel a prophecy for the method of awakening those dry bones.

The hand of the LORD was upon me, and carried me out in the spirit of the LORD, and set me down in the midst of the valley which [was] full of bones, (2) And caused me to pass by them round about: and, behold, [there were] very many in the open valley; and, lo, [they were] very dry. (3) And he said unto me, Son of man, can these bones live? And I answered, O Lord GOD, thou knowest. (4) Again he said unto me, Prophesy upon these bones, and say unto them, O ye dry bones, hear the word of the LORD. (5) Thus saith the Lord GOD unto these bones; Behold, I will cause breath to enter into you, and ye shall live: (6) And I will lay sinews upon you, and will bring up flesh upon you, and cover you with skin, and put breath in you, and ye shall live; and ye shall know that I [am] the LORD. (7) So I prophesied as I was commanded: and as I prophesied, there was a noise, and behold a shaking, and the bones came together, bone to his bone. (8) And when I beheld, lo, the sinews and the flesh came up upon them, and the skin covered them above: but [there was] no breath in them. (9) Then said he unto me, Prophesy unto the wind, prophesy, son of man, and say to the wind, Thus saith the Lord GOD; Come from the four winds, O breath, and breathe upon these slain, that they may live. (10) So I prophesied as he commanded me, and the breath came into them, and they lived, and stood up upon their feet, an exceeding great army (Ezekiel 37:1-10).

I arrived at Bishkek, Kyrgyzstan, early Tuesday morning prepared to use prophecy to attempt to awaken the dry bones of the Muslim mindset. The meetings opened Sabbath night so I had some time to get over jet-lag and see that all of the plans were in place. The banners we had asked to have painted were not started; they had been forgotten about. But God worked miracles and we had first-class picture banners ready and hanging by Friday afternoon. During our pre-meeting with the conference officials, one young minister commented to me about the up-coming meetings. He said that he did not know how I expected to reach the Muslims, since he had used the latest computer technology and could not hold the Muslims in the meetings for more than a few nights. This is typical of the reports I was receiving, when talking about the work with Muslims. There are giants in the land and we are not able to take it. The God of heaven gave me perfect peace and I believed God would see us through.

My friend, Jack, who had been stationed in Central Asia for a year, pulled me aside before the pre-meeting to tell me a story from a previous evangelistic series held eight months earlier. Jack and the evangelist for those meetings conversed about many subjects, including the various problems the evangelist encountered. He told how an older minister had prayer for that evangelistic series on opening night, and in his prayer preached a sermon about Jesus Christ. Jack suggested to me to not let this individual pray, as all of the Muslims attending that series of meetings left after the first night, never to return. This same older minister asked me if I would let him have opening prayer. Even though he was an official in the conference, I politely declined and said I had it already taken care of. The Lord had to keep me on alert because the battle was raging all around us.

There was one understanding the Lord had given me years ago that has been fixed in my mind, while we were translating

Bible studies for Russia in 1989. Prophecy was the message that drove the "Midnight Cry" of Miller and his associates. I grew to believe it will be prophecy that God uses to drive the "Loud Cry" (Revelation 19:10) of the final movement before the second coming of Jesus.

For three months prior to leaving, I spent hours each day putting the thoughts and Biblical beliefs onto paper in sermon format. With each sermon topic, I brought the relevant Qur'an texts into the sequence of Bible verses I planned on using. I used the Qur'an extensively to establish the bridge, or starting point, between it and the Bible.

As we approached the opening night, I wondered what the attendance would be. All of our advertising had been designed to attract the Muslim mind. When I arrived, the television advertising was in place and being broadcast twelve times a day on all three television stations. Because newspapers are affordable to only the wealthy, it was decided not to advertise that way. Handbills, which had been delivered door to door, and the TV advertisements were the only methods we used. In my pre-meeting, I was told the TV advertising would be stopped once the meetings began. I asked how much the TV advertising cost per week for all three stations; I was told it was $184 per week. When it was converted into US dollars, I told them to keep the advertising in place and working until I told them to stop. We ran the advertising for the next two weeks of the meetings and it netted large results. New people were coming every night. The first two nights we had standing room only and then we settled into a full house almost every night.

After two nights, I wanted more chairs brought in, but the church folk were reluctant to do this. I perceived they felt the crowd was soon to leave and they did not want to return all the chairs. Jack and I were staying at the conference office apartment about twenty minutes away and the church there had extra chairs we could use, if we just hauled them over to the meeting site. So we arranged for the conference van to do the hauling for us and the problem was solved.

We started our meetings each night at 6 p.m. As we drove to the Cultural Center meeting site, I was eager to get

107

started. We arrived early, had prayer with the supporting staff and waited. This waiting was hard to do, but remember "the patience of the saints."

The building was all set, the 2300-day banner, which included a Muslim timeline, was hung high on the back wall. The banner was impressive, stretching twenty-five feet long and five feet high. Everything was written in Russian and it remained in place throughout the series, as we used it every night. Each night I used different banners depicting the books of Daniel and Revelation. When that night's presentation was completed, I moved those banners to the side walls; so before the meetings were completed, we had all the banners of prophecy from Daniel and Revelation hanging on the walls side by side. I found myself constantly referring to the banners each night and the people's heads would turn to look. That first night, we had the Daniel 2 image hung along with the 2300-day banner. I believe these banner pictures will be etched in the Muslim attendee's minds forever by God's Holy Spirit.

As is my custom when I do evangelistic meetings, I will not look to see how full the seats are; I leave that for God to handle. With the way the hall was built, it was not possible to enter from a side door easily, so I sat on the front row in prayer. When the time came for the introduction to start, I got up and walked to the lectern and turned and faced a standing-room, overflow crowd. The God of heaven had fulfilled beyond my wildest thought possible, a full house with folks looking for seats.

At the first meeting I told the story of why I had come back to Central Asia. It was because two years before I had seen the mausoleum of the Prophet Daniel in Samarkand, Uzbekistan. I explained to the attendees that the prophecies of Daniel foretold what was going to happen in the world right up to the very end. I explained to them that I was a Seventh-day Adventist. I told them I worshiped the same God Abraham worshiped. This was important to clarify, because Islam believes Christians pray to Jesus. But who did Jesus teach us to pray to in Matthew 6:9-13 (Lord's Prayer)? He taught us to pray to God or the Father. You may not think this is a big difference, but he Bible shows us the right way. The reason I did that was o show I was not a Christian in the conventional Muslim ense of understanding. In brief, a Muslim understands that Christian eats pig, drinks alcohol, gambles, worships three Gods and participates in open adultery, because this is what hey see from Western culture, movies and television. The first hing I tried to do was to show them I was not one of those ypical "Hollywood Christians." I did not refer to myself as Christian in any of these meetings; it was always as a Seventh-day Adventist. These statements were made in the first ew minutes of the opening meeting. While I spoke through translator, we had another pastor who would read the Bible ind Qur'an verses as we came to them.

At the end of the first night, there were two men who remained until most people had left, then they approached the ranslator and me. The one man reached into his suit pocket ind pulled out his police ID, stating he was a major and his issociate was his lieutenant. He said he was from the Religious Secret Police in Bishkek and it was his job to attend every religious meeting to see what was going on and what was being taught. He was very gracious and said that of all the religious meetings he has to attend, the meeting he had just sat through was the most balanced he ever attended. He went on to explain how some of the Islamic meetings in the city were preaching nothing but hate and rebellion. But he mentioned over and over again how well this meeting promoted balance. He and his lieutenant spent over 30 minutes visiting with me.

Early in the first week, a handsome couple in their thirties came up after the meeting. The husband had been crying; he asked me through the translator if it was possible for a Muslim to have salvation. I paused as the translation was given to me and said yes to his question; I then encouraged them to come back for the next meeting. This couple contacted our Bible worker staff after the meetings were completed and became members of the Seventh-day Adventist Church. As the meetings continued, I started to notice more and more people weeping in their seats as the truth of the Word flowed over them.

As we drove back to our apartment after the first meeting
I was thrilled with the attendance. Instantly, doubt crept back
into my mind to tempt me. I wondered how many would come
back for the next night's meeting. Even though our team was
very encouraged, inwardly I wondered just how many would
return. The second meeting was blessed with even more stand
ing than during the first night. By the third night, attendance
started to stabilize. A large crowd was seated, and yet there
were still some standing.

After the second night's meeting, I noticed a young lady
working her way through the crowd toward me. She was com
ing with a purpose in mind. When she came closer to me, she
got the translator's eye and asked me if I believed in dreams
from Allah. As I was gracefully picking my way through that
question, she started to tell me what she had seen earlier in the
day. She had been taking a nap on the couch in her apartment
the television was on and our streamer ads were playing. As
she read the message for our meetings, she said God had spo
ken to her to get up and get going to these meetings. She said
"Do you believe that I was told to come here?" I explained
that it was Allah telling her to attend. Stories like these really
lifted our spirits.

Earlier, before the meetings had started, my printer failed
to work and I had to purchase a new one on Friday, just before
Sabbath. On Sabbath morning, before the first meeting, my
computer locked up and would not run at all. I admit that I am
not a computer whiz and needed help from God. After prayer
the Lord provided the miracle to encourage His servants. My
friend, Jack, who had spent the last year in Central Asia, was with
me at the conference apartment. Before he left for Central Asia
I had purchased a used computer for him, identical to the one I
used. Several months before, his original battery rapidly dete
riorated and I had sent him a replacement to keep him on line
He just happened to have that old battery and when I inserted
it, immediately my computer fired up and worked fine. It was
just a reminder that we were in a spiritual battle each day.

On one particularly dark night, near the beginning of
our evening's presentation, the electricity for the district went
110

ut. To understand the situation, our meetings were held in he Cultural Center, located just blocks away from the largest ower plant in the country. Expecting the devil to attack us t each and every opportunity, I continued to speak in pitch lackness while our assistants found a few candles to light. Ay presentation that evening made reference to the statue f Daniel 2. The audience looked to their right as I pointed o the wall, where, hidden by the darkness, the banner of the tatue hung. As the candles brought light to a darkened room, o the Holy Spirit was bringing light to their minds, and they vere seeing the light of God's truths. Their minds remained mprinted by the vivid banners they saw portrayed each night n the walls.

As we started our second week, I noticed fewer people vere standing and we were starting to have a few chairs that vere not being used. I inquired as to what could be the problem. After some checking, we found out that it was the time or Muslims to go on the Hajj. The Hajj is the trip to Mecca, vhich a good Muslim is expected to make once in a lifetime, f they can afford the cost. Most Muslims do not go on this rip each year. For the ones who stay behind, it is like a big east, lasting for about four days. Once this time of celebration was over, the crowd came back and we had standing oom only again.

Chapter 16

People Stories of the Meetings

"The Hearing Challenged"

When the opening night came, our meeting hall was filled and people were jostling for seats with the good standing places quickly taken. Right behind where I sat on the front row, there were about four rows of deaf Muslims who came to listen to our message. When my translator whispered to me what was happening, I wondered what we would do since we had no signer and I did not know how to obtain one. But the Lord had it all worked out. The deaf families brought their children who could hear and they signed to the parents. As each night's meeting progressed, the children would be like a tag team, when one got tired, they would motion to one of the other children who would jump up and start signing and not miss a word. These were people who were not familiar with spiritual terminology at all. When a phrase or word was spoken that the signer did not understand, they would sign quickly back and forth amongst themselves to come to an agreement on what was in question. Occasionally, the signer would stop and turn to my translator for clarification. It was interesting to see the deaf people signing within their group when a point was in question as I was speaking. Once the meeting routine was found, it all flowed very well. It sounds disruptive, but the hour proceeded smoothly and Allah blessed. One of the deaf young men, in his late teens, was really being touched by what he was hearing and spoke with me about his convictions. He said he was going to tell his family about his desires to follow the message of truth. He never came back and we never heard from him again; we tried to locate him, but were never able. Since our Bible workers could not sign, he fell through the cracks. Oh how I have learned from my failures.

"The Grandmothers"

Early in the first week of the meetings, two grandmo-therly types began attending faithfully each night with their grandchildren. As the meetings progressed, these two ladies realized that we were not attacking Islam, but using the Qur'an in a positive way to point to the Bible. Each evening before the meeting started, we met in the back room for prayer with the staff, where we discussed the progress of the regular attendees. Here I gave an overview of the night's subject. There was a knock on the door; it was these two ladies and they asked if they could come in. We welcomed them in and they spoke to me through the translator, asking if we would pray for their husbands and children to also find the truths we were sharing. We bowed with them and had prayer, offering their requests to God for His will for their salvation. Each night they came faithfully, smiling and greeting our staff.

As the meetings progressed, I was ready to show how Muhammad fell (Revelation 9:1) and how God used Islam after he died. I knew it would be a hard meeting and we would need the presence of God as our Protector that night. I had a friend of mine in Washington State who knew when I was going to be presenting this topic, and he emailed me and encouraged me not to show in the meetings that Muhammad fell or I would lose them. However, I decided to proceed. That night, as I sat in my normal front-row seat looking ahead and praying, I felt a tap on my shoulder. As I turned to see who it was, it was a greeter with one of the grandmothers and she had a smile all over her face. My translator, who was sitting beside me, told me that she thanked us for our prayers, because her husband was with her this night. In one of our previous visits, she told me her husband had forbidden her to come to the meetings, but she would sneak out of the house and get her grandchil-dren and come anyway. Now he was here, a miracle in itself. I got up and followed her over to her husband and shook his hand and greeted him. He did not make eye contact with me and only grunted when it was translated, but at least he was here to listen.

113

I now had a decision to make – was I going to proceed with my planned presentation of showing how Muhammad fell? As I was thinking about all this, I looked at my watch and it was two minutes to six and the meeting was about to begin. I told my translator to have everyone, even the greeters at the door, meet in the prayer room. With everyone in the prayer room, I explained what had just taken place. I said God has answered the prayers of one of the grandmothers and her husband was with her. I was also aware how a Muslim divorce works; all the husband has to do is say something like I divorce you three times and it is all over. I did not want that to happen or worse. I went around the room and asked for opinion and comment, knowing the time was ready to begin the meeting. Everyone agreed, except one person; but after prayer, he was willing to go on with the new plan. Now I had to make up a completely different presentation in the time it takes to walk thirty feet, but the Lord never let me miss a beat. "He" put together a whole new presentation with Qur'an and Bible verses and it just flowed like it had been rehearsed. I have been asked if I ever went back and gave that night's presentation on the failure of Muhammad. I never did. As I prayed and thought about it, I realized that information would come out on its own as a Muslim came to understand the faith of the Word as he grew spiritually. After the meetings were finished and I returned home, these two grandmothers came looking for our church and are now Seventh-day Adventists. At this writing, they have not been cast out of their homes by their families. Praise Allah!

"The Arabs are Coming!"

As I arrived at the meeting location the third evening, all the Bible workers were buzzing around. I asked what all the activity was about. They said the Arabs are coming. I asked "What do you mean, the Arabs are coming?" I was told that our lead Bible worker, a young lady, had gone to the local Arabic university and asked the faculty to attend our meetings. Everyone was just thrilled and they were praying to God and praising His name. I had to act like I was thrilled also, but knew this could be trouble. I did not want to get into an open discussion with Arab clerics or Imams at this point in time. I went to my seat on the first row and started to pray for deliverance. I knew my only defense was to leave it to my heavenly Father. As I stood up to begin the meeting, I noticed that five Arab men had come in and were sitting to my left, near the rear. I could not get any eye contact with them. After the meeting, they left without any comment, and everyone wondered if they would come back. The next night, two came back and they attended much of the series.

The night I introduced the Sin-bearer and the story of the sanctuary, I noticed a little change in their facial expressions. I spent the whole evening on the work of the lamb and what it foreshadowed. I even knelt on the floor as if I had a lamb and how I would have confessed my sin over the head of the lamb, if I had lived in the time of Moses. I explained how I, as the sinner, would have to kill the lamb with a knife. My sin forced me to kill the lamb, if I wanted forgiveness.

After the close of the meeting, the two Arabs went right to the sanctuary banner hanging on the front wall and spent their entire time looking at the painting of the most holy place of the sanctuary. They got close and just stared, putting their hands on the painting of the holy place. Then they just turned around and left without making any eye contact. By now, it had almost become a game to see if I could get a response from them. They came night after night as I went through Daniel 7, 8, 9 and portions of 11 and 12. We also covered portions of Revelation 8-14, 18, 20, and 21. We covered all aspects of Rome in Bible prophecy, using an Islamic understanding where applicable. The two remaining Arabs sat through it all.

The night I covered the Sabbath as the seal of Allah was the night the Arabs came alive. When western evangelists make the point about the Sabbath being the seal of God, we use the picture of a seal, impressed at the end of a document or something similar. We point out that the name, title and territory give the authority to the seal. I knew I had to do better than that in the Muslim culture, or the point would not be made about the Sabbath. As I was praying in my sermon-preparation time, the thought came to me to use Muhammad in making my point. When I do meetings of any kind, I try to refrain from asking questions that require an audible answer; I do not want anyone to be embarrassed by giving the wrong answer, but I still want their minds to be challenged. I felt that I needed to take the chance, even though I was using a translator and the effect could be lost in translation. When I came to the seal of the Sabbath, this is what I said, "Islam teaches that Muhammad has a seal on him, why?" As the translation was given it seemed like the wait was forever. Then hands started to pop up and voices started to speak out in Russian. They were saying the right answer, "Muhammad was the last prophet and he is sealed as the last one." They made my point that the last has the seal. Within Islam, the belief is that Muhammad has a seal because he was the last prophet. The point I was attempting to make was the Sabbath is the last day in the weekly cycle, so it would be the sealed day. The act of worshiping on the seventh day, keeping the seventh day as did Abraham and Ishmael, made them think. I went on to explain it was not just a legalistic day, but a day that brought rest to the soul. In the Qur'an, Muhammad chastises the Jews as Sabbathbreakers. Sura 4:47 says, "O ye people of the Book! believe in what We have (now) revealed confirming what was (already) with you before We change the face and fame of some (of you) beyond all recognition and turn them hindwards or curse them as We cursed the Sabbath-breakers: for the decision of Allah must be carried out." This Qur'an verse is very plain, because it shows the Sabbath had been from before and curses are on those who break the Sabbath.

At this point in the meeting, I took a chance where I could lose everyone, but felt it the right time to make the point. I said, "I believe Muhammad was a Sabbathkeeper, or how could Muhammad criticize someone for not obeying the Sabbath, and I do not believe Muhammad was a hypocrite?" There was dead silence in the room; I let it settle in a moment. If I were challenged by the audience on this point, they would be in essence saying that Muhammad is a hypocrite and any self-respecting Muslim would never say that. I know many western evangelists would make a call of hands or standing to commit to the Sabbath, but I felt this would end our discussion before it was time. I had many more things to present, and as this was the first time these people had heard the truths of the Bible tied to the Qur'an, I knew I was pushing the line on this one.

As the meeting closed, the two Arabs jumped to their feet and came straight for me. They were both smiling as they reached for my hand to shake it and asked why I had not become a Muslim. That was the first time someone had asked that question, but not the last. The first thing one of the Arabs said was that Islam keeps no day holy; I acknowledged that point with them. The next thing they said to me was astounding. "We were taught in Jordan, as small boys, about the little horn power, just as you have presented here." I asked if they had understood the points on Rome as I had given them and they both said, "Yes." We talked about the aspects of Rome and the United States and it resonated with them in the affirmative. The Arabs were now my friends, because I had given them the truth of the Bible as the Holy Spirit directed. When we teach the prophecies of Daniel and Revelation to western audiences, and it is a condition of our faith, why not teach the same to audiences in the Muslim world?

"Perfect Object Lesson"

One day while the meetings were going on, the "perfect crime" was committed by my friend Jack's translator, Natasha. The pair had been driving around in the city, earlier during the day, for mission work. Natasha had neglected to buckle her seat belt and when they were stopped by the police, she was fined about one dollar in the local currency. Natasha had no money and could not pay the fine; she needed Jack to pay the penalty for her. That night, my presentation was about the need for a Sin-bearer, for someone to pay the price for our sins. I could not have asked for a better example of the work of the Messiah. Just as Jack had to pay the penalty for his trusted translator's failure to buckle up, so the Messiah had to pay the penalty for our sin to restore us back to the sinless condition for heaven, because of His love for us. In the Muslim mindset,

117

they have no method to be restored to this condition, because of their beliefs. This simple object lesson was easily understood by everyone in attendance that evening. Muslims have need of a Sin-bearer.

"Rough-Looking Fellows"

As I stood up to begin the first night's meeting, I noticed a pair of pretty tough-looking characters sitting in the back row. They wore the old gangster-type hats. They were taller and bigger than almost everyone else I had seen in Kyrgyzstan. They were not just sitting and listening; they were whispering back and forth, leaning forward and putting their hands on the chair in front of them; they were in constant movement. One would get up and leave and then come back.

Opening night I was keeping my eye on almost everything going on around me, because we just did not know what might happen. As the meetings continued, one man stopped coming, but the bigger one still attended. He was becoming calmer as the meetings continued. I also noticed that there was another man who had started to sit by him each night. This man had tried to convince me of many far-out ideas on many topics of false faith. I knew this man was filling this seeker's head full of untruths. When I understood that this was going on, I instructed our Bible workers, male and female, to move in and surround this new seeker of truth wherever he sat, and not let this other man sit close to him. The Bible workers did their job and that took care of the problem. It was amazing to see the power of the Word of God make this man calmer and calmer as the truths were explained each night. He did not miss a night as I recall. As the meetings had been extended to three weeks and time was winding down, it became apparent that he was serious about the truths he was hearing. If this young man, a native Kyrgyz, became a Seventh-day Adventist, we could train him and place him back in the field, speaking the native Kyrgyz language.

After the meetings were completed, he did become a Seventh-day Adventist. Everyone in the Kyrgyz conference speaks

Russian, but no one picked up on the fact this young man spoke only Russian. His family had not spoken their native tongue in the home as they wanted to be Russian speaking. We are still "waiting" for more male Kyrgyz nationals who speak the Kyrgyz language to accept the message and become workers. There are a few older Seventh-day Adventist Kyrgyz national females, one of whom is said to be able to translate from Russian to Kyrgyz. The wait for workers goes on; the fields are ripe for the harvest, but where are the reapers?

The Central Asian Conference Muslim leader tracked this young man down where he lived and later told me an amazing story. He would leave his home and walk two or three miles to get to the bus stop. He lived on the far side of the city, out in the country. In order for him to be at the meeting by six o'clock, he left his home around three thirty each afternoon. When the meetings were over at a little past seven, he would head home. Some of the buses had stopped running by this time, as he worked his way across the city. He would arrive home between eleven and midnight. In American cities there are street lights at night; but in the former USSR, there aren't any street lights, except in the downtown areas. Thus, he was in the dark on those cold winter nights as he traveled home. When I heard this story, I knew that God was completely in charge, confirming our Father in heaven had given His people the right message for Islam. As the pastor visited the home of this young man and his family, he inquired if the parents were concerned their son was coming to meetings about the Bible, and then later his decision to become a follower of the Word. The parents said it was their son's decisions and they would support him in that. This was a broad-minded Muslim family. Praise Allah!

The "White-haired Lady" and Trouble

After getting acclimated to the meeting routine each night, you start noticing different people and their actions. We soon recognized that we had perhaps ten Seventh-day Adventists scattered around in our group, outside of the staff. Later, in the first week after the meeting was over, my translator and I were surrounded with Muslims waiting to ask questions. As I was listening to a question being asked of my translator in Russian, I noticed this slightly built, white-haired lady bent over at the waist, pushing through the crowd, and coming into the center of our circle by elbowing everyone who did not give her the right of way. As she was elbowing her way through, I thought, this is a rather rude person. When she got in front of the translator, she straightened up and interrupted everyone with her words, shaking her finger in my translator's face. She said, "When are you going to tell these Muslims that Jesus Christ is the Son of God?" I have never been a boxer and taken a punch, but I took this hit and tried to show no emotion either way. I knew she was trying to help me out, but did not understand what she had just done to God's message. I turned to the lady and looked at her, studied her for a short period of time and then turned to my translator and asked for the next question from the Muslims. She retired from the face of the conflict and left. But she did return the next night and did not miss another meeting. There were no more outbursts from her. What I did not know, however, was what was going on behind the scenes at the conference office!

We were having each night's talk put on audio cassettes so they could be shared with others after we left. Apparently the next day, this "white-haired lady" and her supporters were in the conference president's office demanding that these meetings be stopped. I was charged with not presenting Jesus Christ to the people. The leadership of the church, being busy, was unable to attend each night on a regular basis during the three week series. On the last Thursday I was to be in Kyrgyzstan, had a meeting with the conference leadership. They were more than kind and expressed their thanks to both Jack and me in what we were trying to do. They said they had been listening to each presentation on cassette tape. Then they told me the story of the "white-haired lady" and how she demanded I be stopped, so they were "forced" to get the tapes and listen in the conference office to the previous night's talk. They said they had nothing but the utmost support for our effort and that we should continue.

"Chinese Dungi or Wigger People"

The third week had started and the things that needed to e done before I left were pushing me every waking moment. had been away from home four weeks in the dead of the Minnesota winter. The computer email ability was off and on t best at an internet café, when I could be there. The meeting lace was packed and crowded each night — the people coming late having to stand. It was great to see people standing o hear the truth in a dark land.

At the start of the last week, we had about seven or eight lew people come in early and get seats near the front. They vere early middle aged and dressed very nicely. After the meeting, they waited for the people to leave, then made a ircle around me. All the men and women had big smiles. One of the ladies spoke to me in perfect English and asked low long I had been speaking in the city? I told her that this vas the last week I was to be there. The group spoke through he English speaker and said that they had been Muslims, out had been convinced from reading the Bible that it was rue. They were not part of any denomination, but were meeting in their homes for the last three years, studying the Bible and worshiping each week. I asked who they were. They explained that they were called "Dungi" or "Wigger", neaning they were Chinese Muslims before they accepted the nessage of the Bible. They asked if I could come and hold a series of meetings in their home. They are still waiting for ny return. Most of them attended the remaining meetings and took notes and shared with the rest of their group each night. They kept asking me if they could get anything written about what we were sharing from the Bible and Qur'an n book form. I sadly told them I did not have anything written, as this was my first experiment with the material we had found in the Bible, Qur'an and world history. It was becoming painfully apparent that this information needed to be in printed format. We now have an understanding of the themes to include in books and tracts to reach the Muslim mind. The book you are reading is a chronicle of finding this information, then seeing if it works. This book attempts to tell the first part of the story.

There are people who are already using the information found in this book who have become effective agents to break down the walls of Muslim misunderstandings of the Bible. The struggles are many; we do not have a good Arabic Bible that is effective in Daniel, Revelation and the Gospels, but this is His work and He knows. We need to keep our Seventh-day Adventist movement moving forward by letting God open the closed doors before us with His word of prophecy; remember Revelation 19:10.

The Last Night

The closing meeting was on Sabbath night. When I realized how the people responded to the truth, I extended the meetings for a week. During that final week, every waking moment was used to create additional presentations for the eastern mindset so it would flow with what they had already been taught. The Lord blessed in a mighty way. It had taken me three months to put together the two-week series, now had to make six more effective presentations in seven days, quickly responding to the audience's desire to know more about the truths of the Bible and history. Again, God is good. We have a bottomless source of the water of life in the Word, or the "Book," as Muhammad would say. I felt we could not stop when such interest was kindled. It was my intention to go for two weeks and use the last week to do visitation and arrange for follow-up with different people. Finally, the closing night came and was met with sadness that the meetings had to end, but happiness for me, because within a few hours I would be on a British Air flight home at 4 am Sunday morning.

The last night I poured out my heart for those Muslim people, who were standing along the side walls and around behind me; you could hardly move it was so crowded. Tears were in the eyes of the Muslims, as I told them about heaven from the "Book" and what we would miss out on if we did not submit to Allah. God moved the people in a mighty way.

hated to leave as I knew what these people needed. They
eeded to be shown the path of Bible truth, the path of Abra-
am's walk with God, his failures and his blessings. Those
lessings are still available to each seeking, spiritual member
f the "children of the East." The closing prayer that night
vas offered by the conference official who wanted to preach
 sermon about Jesus in the opening night's prayer. He could
ow preach his prayer about the Messiah and they would know
vhat it meant and not be offended. The time was now ready
ɔ boldly approach the throne of grace, as it was not the time
ɔ do that at the beginning of the meetings.

> To every [thing there is] a season, and a time to every
> purpose under the heaven: (2) A time to be born, and a
> time to die; a time to plant, and a time to pluck up [that
> which is] planted" (Ecclesiastes 3:1, 2).

After many hugs and handshakes, I left the building for
ne last time. Just three weeks earlier to the very night, we had
tarted with much trust, hope and faith that the information
ve had been shown by God would be a blessing for the Mus-
m people. We acted on conviction that it was correct and it
vould work to reach the heart of a Muslim; and it did just as
God had promised (Matthew 28:18-20).

That last night I only had three hours sleep, as the con-
erence officials were visiting and giving our ministry letters
f support and invitations to return. As I packed up and
ollected my things, my mind was racing with the happen-
ngs of the last four weeks. Going into the meetings, I was
t peace believing that whatever happened, the Lord had led
s into the right information. I pray and prayed that I did
ot abuse or misapply God's truth for this time. That is still
ny prayer as the work continues. We must be open to go
vhere He leads and not be closed to unfolding Bible truth.
ome Seventh-day Adventists are deeply concerned that this
nformation is called "new light" and it does not stand the
est of the Word. I believe that this book shows that it is not
iew light per se, but it shows a clearer understanding from
vhat our Advent pioneers preached. I believe God has given

us a wider grasp of our Bible and a renewed conviction tha
Islam can be reached.

As you read this, you may be asking why I did not pus
for baptisms. My thrust of this effort was to show that propf
ecy will work in the world of Islam. I was under convictio
on that point. Up until the time of these meetings, there we
few Seventh-day Adventists who would feel comfortable wit
this method. In many Muslim countries in the past, some o
the Muslims who became Christians and were baptized lo:
their lives in martyrdom or they had to flee for their lives an
leave the home country in what is called the extraction methoc
The persons who taught them the truth also had to flee fc
their lives as well. The extracted Seventh-day Adventist lose
much of his usefulness as a witness, hindered greatly in h
ability to reach his family and home country for the kingdon
The way to evangelize or reach Islam is a topic of concern i
some areas of our church today. Our church leaders need ot
prayers as they wrestle with the issue of reaching twenty-tw
percent of the world's population. The following chapter a
tempts to show another method, or added understanding t
reach Islam, to accomplish the mission God has given us to g
to the entire world.

Chapter 17

Is There Another Way to Reach Our Brothers and Sisters, the "Children of the East"?

> And he showed me a pure river of water of life, clear as crystal, proceeding out of the throne of God and of the Lamb. (2) In the midst of the street of it, and on either side of the river, [was there] the tree of life, which bare twelve [manner of] fruits, [and] yielded her fruit every month: and the leaves of the tree [were] for the healing of the nations (Revelation 22:1, 2).

The last chapter of Revelation begins with a picture of heaven. John is given a view of the river of life that flows from the throne of God and of the Lamb. The tree of life is pictured as spanning the river of life with twelve manner of fruit, one for each month. The last phrase of the verse tells us that the leaves are for the healing of the nations. As I considered the "healing of the nations" in my study, I asked myself: "What is the meaning of that? What needs healing in heaven? Are not the saints' physical bodies changed in a moment, in the twinkling of an eye'" (1 Corinthians 15:52)? From Philippians 2:5 we know they have the same mind that Jesus had. Revelation 22:2 speaks of "the leaves of the tree [were] for the healing of the nations." This text has a real meaning for anyone working in the Islamic community today. It gives us hope.

The word *contextualization* is a word that seems to evoke strong opinions when seeking ways to reach the heart of Islam. The word *contextualize* means: "To place a word or idea in a particular context." The struggle a Bible believer has is how to give the message of salvation to a Muslim without being killed or having the Muslim seeker killed. This forces anyone who works for the salvation of Islam to adjust the way the message of the Bible is presented. It does not change the message, but simply attempts to present the message in terms and understandings a Muslim can grasp, in an Islamic setting, that will not affect the power of the Word. The charges are easily hurled about in Christian circles that the message has been changed or altered to be made acceptable, when the word contextualize is connected with the Bible. We need only look to Jesus and how He taught about the Godhead; He pointed His followers to the God of heaven. When Paul was in a Jewish community, he presented the truth in a way an honest Jewish seeker could understand. When he was in a Greek community, he presented the truth in a way an honest Gentile seeker could understand. This way of presentation removed the stumbling block from before the seekers so they could hear the plan of salvation. Remember, the leaves are for the healing of the nations and this will take place in heaven. In order to be a servant of the most high God, we will have to lay aside our western religious culture and be a slave for God and do His will to reach the world. Western church culture runs deep, deeper than most of us have ever thought possible. Our Seventh-day Adventist culture will not save anyone, but we need to live and share the culture of Jesus in the Bible, which points us to heaven.

I would propose that the characteristics of the saints who are to be healed by the leaves of the tree of life are those cultural practices that now separate one from another, but not from God. In one of my first forays into the Spanish world, I was kindly asked the question: "What language will we speak in heaven?" My Spanish questioner was not willing to accept my smiling answer that it would be English. This writer knows full well, English will not be spoken in heaven, nor do I believe it will be Spanish. The language will be the language of heaven, whatever that may be.

The American Seventh-day Adventist mindset on the subject of reaching the world with the gospel carries with it a lot of cultural baggage. In many parts of the world, it appears that our message format has great success preparing millions of souls for heaven. Americans, who have not traveled outside the United States, may not perceive how culture affects the message of salvation, as it is given to a foreign audience. The western cultural spin often alters its reception. One of my first confrontations with a foreign Seventh-day Adventist culture was during a trip to Korea in 1986. I was there in November and the weather was cold. My translator and I attended one of our churches on Sabbath. At the front door, I was told to take off my shoes and put them on the men's side of the outer lobby of the church. I had just been confronted with a cultural difference that had an effect on how I was to think and act. Was I being forced to take off my shoes? I do not think so. But, if I had not taken my shoes off, anything that I had to say to that church body would have been altered by their Korean reaction to my American behavior. So, the shoes came off and I remembered that I had better be aware of anything else that I might do to cause a diversion or interfere with the acceptance of my message.

How do our western cultural presentations alter Biblical themes, and how are these cultural practices perceived in the minds of the audience? Are we seeing things only from an American cultural understanding? The Seventh day-Adventists in North America are told the 10/40 window is opening up. The initiative to build places of worship for the people in these cultures has increased our success in the 10/40 window. The Adventist group, "Maranatha," has spearheaded this work and promotes the hands-on type of western evangelism to build churches for the new converts. "Gospel Outreach" puts national workers in those areas where long-term evangelism is needed, to bring more people to the saving truth of the Third Angel's Message. The "Gospel Outreach" form of mission work is being expanded and used often by our church before and after the American evangelistic series. The "Gospel Outreach" team does the pre-work, and many times it becomes a permanent fixture after the American team leaves. They are often successful and I believe the Lord has led in this work.

The 3ABN television network has many inquiries from Muslims in the Middle East; it appears that Muslims are looking for more spiritual information. They are asking for more information on Jesus and the Bible. Sura 43:61 says: "And Jesus shall be a Sign for the coming of the Hour of Judgment therefore have no doubt about the Hour but follow ye Me: this is a Straight Way." The note that accompanies this verse by Yusuf Ali, respected translator of the Qur'an, states: "This is understood to refer to the second coming of Jesus in the Last Days before the Resurrection, when he will destroy the false doctrines that pass under his name, and prepare the way for the universal acceptance of Islam, the Gospel of Unity and Peace, the Straight Way of the Qur'an." Yes, that is right! The Muslim world is looking for the second coming of the same Jesus we are, the same Jesus that the wise men, "children of the East," came to worship. If it shocks you as a Seventh-day Adventist to hear this, it did the same to me when I read it while doing my early research. This shared connection should compel us to examine our hearts to see how our inner souls relate to these latter day "children of the East." If we maintain the same approach to Islam that other denominations use, we will fail to reach them. Our efforts will die with us this side of the Jordan. Bible stories and prophecy need to be a part of our message.

The work goes on, but are we really following the Bible example of taking the gospel to the world, or are we forcing through our western funnel of understanding? At this time in earth's history, we need "Daniels" who will dare to step out and really make an effort to reach Islam, using new methods and approaches. Through Daniel and his three friends' example King Nebuchadnezzar was converted and wrote his inspired account in the book of Daniel. Are Seventh-day Adventists really willing to be a Daniel or do we just want to sing the song about it? The time is right, the fields are ripe for the harvest, but where are the reapers? Where are the combine drivers? If the reapers and combine drivers are perched in front of the TV, looking at the six o'clock news, and not searching the word of God, the harvest will be past, God will not be served and we will be lost.

I have come to know from first-hand experience that per-
nal evangelism and witnessing must come from the heart; it
ust become second nature. Witnessing is not something we
) to do at a certain time each week. It springs from a blessing
· conviction of thankfulness for what God has done for us.
s we take communion we must remember the symbolism
·presented. Receiving the life of Christ into our very heart
id souls, the Holy Spirit can control our actions and thoughts
y His power.

I have written a little in the preceding chapters about what
luslims actually believe. Did you know there are over forty
assages in the Qur'an that speak about Jesus in a positive
ght that we as Seventh-day Adventists can use in sharing
ith a Muslim? In Sura 2:87, it tells about Jesus coming from
od to Mary, his earthly mother. Sura 3:45, 4:157, 171 say that
·sus is the Messiah. Please consider Sura 3:45: "Behold! The
ngels said "O Mary! Allah giveth thee glad tidings of a Word
om Him: his name will be Christ Jesus the son of Mary held
1 honor in this world and the Hereafter and of (the company
f) those nearest to Allah." This Sura tells us that angels told
lary His name and that His name will be an honor in this
·orld and the afterworld. The foundations of truth are in the
)ur'an; they point to the Bible as the "Book." I strongly sug-
·est that we set our "Christian" prejudices aside and see what
ie God of heaven can do for His "children of the East" in the
nal work. Are you and I willing to be His servants and carry
ie message to Islam? Islam is seeking the truths we have in
ie Third Angel's Message. They want to know what is going
) happen, and Revelation has the answer.

The Qur'an has verses that uphold and support the
iith of Seventh-day Adventists and the Bible. I would
ncourage all to use these natural bridges to point to deeper
nderstandings of the Bible for Islam. What would the God
f heaven have us do with the information He has given
) us in this Book? Would He condemn, or speak to the
ommon ground of understanding and build from there?
Ve need to follow His example by His power and submit
) His will to reach the people whose origin stems from

a failure by our spiritual father, Abraham, millennia ag (Galatians 3:29).

I received a phone call from a pastor friend who has bee interested in Islamic work for a long time. He had accompanie me to a Mosque in Hamburg, Germany, as we presented th prophecies of Daniel and Revelation to Muslim scholars, so I understands the roll of Islam in the Bible. In one of his distri churches a member had been carrying on an exchange with Muslim pharmacist. After my pastor friend was introduce he waited for the pharmacist to close his shop, as it was lat As he was waiting, the pharmacist gave my friend a letter I had just received in the mail from another Christian minister. was about the Trinity. When the pharmacy closed, they went a little restaurant to continue visiting. After they were seate the Muslim, thinking my friend was just like most Christian started in against Christians who push the Trinity and want show that Jesus is God before anything else is discussed.

When the Muslim began to tire after about forty-fiv minutes, the pastor told him that the God of the Bible ha blessed the "children of the East" and used them as a deliver for Joseph, when his brothers wanted to kill him. The past explained story after story from the Bible about how God use the "children of the East." The Muslim then began to chang his attitude when he realized he was not being attacked. Whe he found out that Seventh-day Adventists did not eat pork ar abided by the standards of the "Book," he was shocked. Aft more than three hours of sharing, the Muslim said, "You a not like the others."

The pastor used statements from the Qur'an showing th there is a difference between Christians. Sura 3:113 states: "N all of them are alike: of the People of the Book are a portion th stand (for the right); they rehearse the signs of Allah all nig long and then prostrate themselves in adoration." The Bib in Revelation 9:4 explains that there is a difference betwee Christians. Can a Muslim tell the difference between Seventh day Adventist Christians and other Christians? If not, we hav some serious soul searching to do, because God has called us t "higher ground." (see *Review and Herald*, April 26, 1906)

When we share our faith with our Roman Catholic friends, do we discuss those points of doctrine upon which we disagree on our first visit? It is doubtful. If we are willing to use different methods to reach a Christian soul, maybe we should consider doing the same with Muslims. Let us not become known as just another Christian people, but as a people with a message of saving grace for each Muslim with whom we come in contact.

There have been thousands of pages written about the message of salvation to reach the Muslim heart. If we attempt to reach Muslims the same way as in our conventional evangelistic efforts, we may be able to gain a small handful. Once they take a stand and leave Islam, more than likely, they will be cast out of their family and possibly killed. For more information on the viewpoint of the insider movement without disturbing the Muslim culture, I would recommend two books. The first is *Building Bridges* by Fouad Elias Accad, ISBN 0-89109-795-3. The other book is *The Belief of Ismail* by Adan Ibn Ismail (no ISBN number).

The people of the Third Angel's Message have a unique insight into the work of God in prophecy and in the shaping of end-time events. But knowing all of the prophetic understandings will not save us. We must have the blessed hope burning in our hearts. May you and I have the blessed hope each day by His grace.

I trust the ideas presented in this book will challenge you to new understandings about the "children of the East." They are joint heirs of the promises that God gave to Abraham for his heritage. They are to receive every promise, except the new covenant promise. That promise must be accepted the same way we accepted it, individually by faith. As spiritual Israel (Galatians 3:29), we have a sacred work before us. End-time events are unfolding each day. Events in the world are happening that have never happened before; the nations are angry (Revelation 11:18). We need to "Get Ready," "Get Ready," "Get Ready," for the coming judgment of the world; are you and I ready now?

Author's Notes

It is my sincere hope that you have been blessed and hav understood the many points included in these pages. Thi book has been written to demonstrate that God has not left H church without instruction in these days leading up to the Sur day law and to His second coming. Our understanding of th seventh trumpet-third woe is not yet complete; this is on-goin and still unfolding to His people. But we must remember tha the unfolding will not change or do away with what God ha revealed to us in the past. The key point I want to leave wit you is this: Islam, the "wild man" side, was used by God t bring judgment on the predominant apostate Christian churc of the Middle Ages, and He will again use Islam's "wild man side to bring judgment against the new beast power of Rev elation 13:11. If we, as Seventh-day Adventists, continue t maintain blind patriotic support for the power of Revelatio 13:11, as it is transitioning into the power that will cause th world to worship the first beast of Revelation 13:1-10, we wi fail in perfecting our characters for heaven by the power of th Holy Spirit. We have the power and promise of God knockin at the door of our hearts (Revelation 3:20). Will we let Hir in and partake of His Spirit that will transform our souls int His life (Philippians 2:5)?

The answer to understanding prophecy is to conside how "God has led us in the past" (*Review and Herald*, March 1 1895). This will give us the insight necessary to be open to H leading by the Holy Spirit as end-time events unfold aroun us. We must not let the evening news reports influence ou understanding of these end-time closing events, as the worl sees them. The prophecies we have been given by God in th past will give us the needed insight to understand the even the news is reporting. God has many things to give us as tim continues to unfold, but any new understanding will never d away with the foundation pillars of faith our pioneers unde stood and wrote about.

Each one of us needs to be asking the question: How can Islam effectively be reached with the gospel? Before we can go before anyone and witness we must have the correct Biblical understandings and be able to share it in the right cultural method. I would encourage a study of the four gospels on how Jesus progressively moved forward with His message. When He met the woman by the well, she was approached differently than the Jews were. We must tailor our message the way Jesus would. Much of Islam, in different parts of the world, is based on tradition and folk-Islam; each Muslim group must be reached with different methods, but the same truth from the Word will be successful and God will bless.

God has not abandoned us to the storms of strife; He is the anchor, which cannot be moved. Will we let our anchor hold, or will we pull it up and look at it to see if it is still attached to the anchor chain? It will hold, if we seek repentance at the foot of the cross and look to the sanctuary in heaven, by faith, for the working of Jesus, Who took on humanity for you and me (Psalms 77:13, Matthew 10:23, *Desire of Ages*, page 25).

I will stand upon my watch, and set me upon the tower, and will watch to see what he will say unto me, and what I shall answer when I am reproved. (2) And the LORD answered me, and said, Write the vision, and make [it] plain upon tables, that he may run that readeth it. (3) For the vision [is] yet for an appointed time, but at the end it shall speak, and not lie: though it tarry, wait for it; because it will surely come, it will not tarry. (4) Behold, his soul [which] is lifted up is not upright in him: but the just shall live by his faith. (Habakkuk 2:1-4)

Maranatha!

2300-Day Time Line

B.C.

457—Starting point for the twenty-three hundred year prophecy of Daniel 8:14. See Ezra 6:14; 7:12–16.

408—The year that the restoration of Jerusalem was completed in fulfillmen of Daniel 9:25.

168—Pagan Rome conquers Macedonia, beginning its rise to power.

31—Pagan Rome conquers Egypt at the battle of Actium fulfilling Daniel 8:9, and beginning the three-hundred and sixty year time-prophecy in which pagan Rome would rule the world supremely as predicted in Daniel 11:24.

A.D.

27—Jesus is baptized in fulfillment of Daniel 9:25.

31—Jesus is crucified in fulfillment of Daniel 9:26, 27.

34—The Jews are divorced from God and the gospel goes to the Gentiles in fulfillment of Daniel 9:24 and Matthew 18:21, 22.

70—Jerusalem destroyed in fulfillment of Daniel 9:26.

330—Pagan Rome moves its capital to Constantinople, fulfilling the three-hundred and sixty years of supremacy as the fourth kingdom of Bible proph ecy in fulfillment of Revelation 13:2 and Daniel 8:11; 11:24, 27, 29.

496—Clovis, king of France, converts to Catholicism and dedicates his throne and military to the papal power, thus beginning the work of remov-ing the three horns of Daniel 7:20, 24 in fulfillment of Revelation 13:2 and Daniel 8:12; 11:31.

508—All religious and military restraint against the Papacy has been removed in fulfillment of 2 Thessalonians 2:6, 7. The twelve hundred and ninety year time-prophecy of Daniel 12:11 begins.

533—Justinian turns his authority over to the Papacy by identifying the pop as the "corrector of heretics and head of all churches" in fulfillment of Rev-elation 13:2 and Daniel 7:25, as the fourth trumpet of Revelation 8 comes to a conclusion.

538—The Goths, last of the three horns, flee the city of Rome in March, beginning the twelve hundred and sixty years of papal rule in fulfillment of Daniel 7:20, 24, 25; 12:7 and Revelation 11:2, 3; 12:6, 14; 13:5.

Children of the East/Islamic Time Line

A.D.

70—Mohammed born. Revelation 9:1

•22—Fifth trumpet-first woe begins.

•32—Mohammed dies and is succeeded by Abubekr.

ıly 27, 1299—The one hundred fifty year time-prophecy of the fifth trum-
•et in Revelation 9:5, 10, begins at the battle of Nicomedia. Islam fulfils the
•rophecy of Revelation 9:11, later confirmed by Martin Luther in his day
ınder the sixth trumpet-second woe.

ıly 27, 1449—Constantine, the last Roman emperor, refuses to ascend the
hrone without permission of the Ottoman Turks, thus bringing the fifth
rumpet-first woe to a conclusion and beginning the sixth trumpet-second
voe. The three hundred ninety-one year, fifteen day time-prophecy of Rev-
 lation 9:15 begins.

798—Atheistic France takes the pope captive, thus delivering the deadly
vound of Revelation 13:3, 10 and Daniel 7:26; 11:40, thus concluding the
welve hundred and sixty years of papal rule. The twelve hundred and ninety
year time-prophecy of Daniel 12:11 is also fulfilled.

August 11, 1840—The sixth trumpet-second woe concludes at the collapse
•f the Ottoman empire in fulfillment of Revelation 9:15, and thus begins the
irst angel's message in fulfillment of Revelation 10:1-4; 14:6, 7.

842—The second angel's message of Revelation 14:8 begins when the
•rganized churches close their doors to the Millerite Movement.

843—The first disappointment for the Millerites arrives and the thirteen
ıundred and thirty-five year time-prophecy of Daniel 12:12 is fulfilled.

)ctober 22, 1844—The Great Disappointment arrives in fulfillment of Dan-
el 8:14, and the "mystery of God" begins in fulfillment of Revelation 10:7
ıs the seventh trumpet-third woe begins to sound in fulfillment of Revelation
:2, 6; 11:14-19.

anuary 1984—Ronald Reagan appoints an ambassador to the Vatican pro-
•hetically identifying that Protestant America has begun to fulfill its role as
'the false prophet" of Revelation 16:13-16; 13:11-17 and that America has
ormed the alliance of Daniel 11:40.

;eptember 11, 2001—Radical Islam begins the final earthly movements of
he seventh trumpet-third woe in fulfillment of the prophecy of Ishmael's
lescendants in Genesis 16:12, while striking the two horns of strength of the
alse prophet—military and economic. The third woe will follow in succes-
ion to the first two woes in order and increasing magnitude.

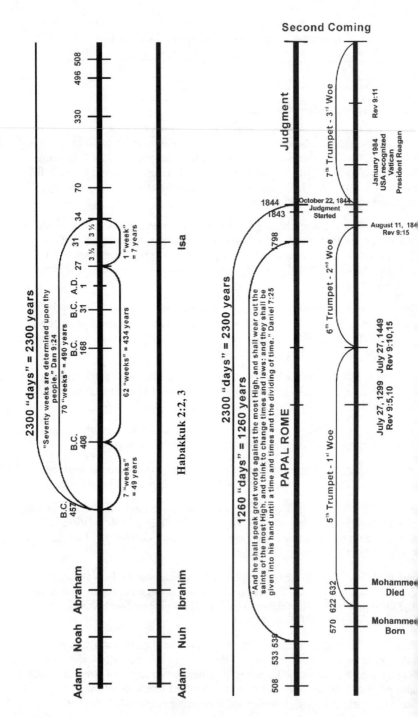

Second Coming

2300 "days" = 2300 years

"Seventy weeks are determined upon thy people." Dan 9:24

70 "weeks" = 490 years

B.C. 457	B.C. 408	B.C. 168	B.C. 31	B.C. A.D. 1	27	31	34	70	330	496 508

7 "weeks" = 49 years

62 "weeks" = 434 years

1 "week" = 7 years

3½   3½

Habakkuk 2:2, 3

Adam   Noah   Abraham   Isa

Adam   Nuh   Ibrahim

2300 "days" = 2300 years

1260 "days" = 1260 years

"And he shall speak great words against the most High, and shall wear out the saints of the most High, and think to change times and laws: and they shall be given into his hand until a time and times and the dividing of time." Daniel 7:25

PAPAL ROME

Judgment

508	533 539		1798	1843 1844

October 22, 1844
Judgment Started

5th Trumpet - 1st Woe

6th Trumpet - 2nd Woe

7th Trumpet - 3rd Woe

570 622 632

Mohammed Born

Mohammed Died

July 27, 1299
Rev 9:5,10

July 27, 1449
Rev 9:10,15

August 11, 1840
Rev 9:15

January 1984
USA recognized
Vatican
President Reagan

Rev 9:11

136

Map Explanations

On the following pages are two maps displaying the expansion of Islam across Europe and Asia. The map called "The Growth of the Ottoman Empire" shows the extent of Islamic (Ottoman) power at the time of the Reformation continuing to the Twentieth Century. It is interesting to note the extent of conquest into Europe to deliver and protect the young Reformation at the time of Luther.

The map called "The Growth of the Islamic World" shows the extent of the Islamic expansion within one hundred seventeen (117) years after Mohammad's death. It covered all the way from southern France, down through the Iberian Peninsula, across North Africa, through what we call the Holy Land today, and into Central Asia up to the mountains of Western China. A crescent of containment was placed around the expanding Holy Roman Empire, which remained in place more or less until the Reformation time of Martin Luther. From the 1530's it started its decline, which continued for the next three (3) plus centuries.

Maps Courtesy of Paul Lunde, *Islam: Faith • Culture • History*,
D & K Publishing

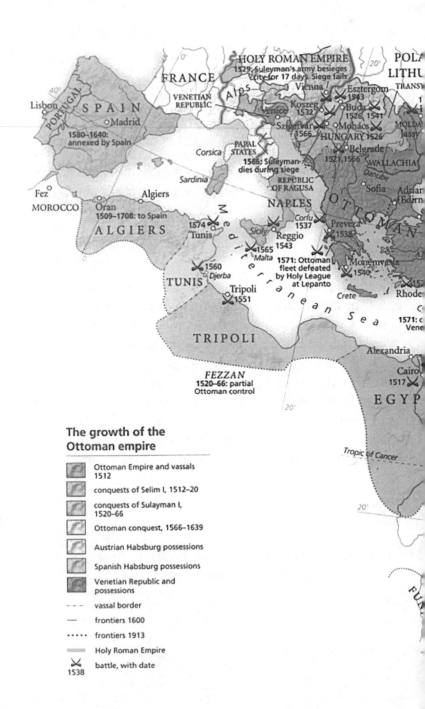

The growth of the
Ottoman empire

Ottoman Empire and vassals
1512

conquests of Selim I, 1512–20

conquests of Sulayman I,
1520–66

Ottoman conquest, 1566–1639

Austrian Habsburg possessions

Spanish Habsburg possessions

Venetian Republic and
possessions

- - -   vassal border

———   frontiers 1600

· · · · ·   frontiers 1913

▬▬▬   Holy Roman Empire

✗   battle, with date
1538

138

POLAND-
LITHUANIA
TRANSYLVANIA   Kiev

1620
Khotin
×1538
MOLDAVIA   Bender
Jassy   JEDISAN
CHIA
KHANATE
OF THE
CRIMEA   Azov
Kaffa
(Kefe)
Adrianople
(Edirne)   Black Sea
Constantinople
RUSSIAN
EMPIRE

CIRCASSIA
Caucasus

Astrakhan
1556: annexed
by Russian Empire

GEORGIAN
STATES   ×1578   ×1578
Derbent
Trebizond
Amasya   Tiflis   Ganja   Baku
N EMPIRE   Erzurum   Kars   ×1588   ×1583
ANATOLIA   ×1578
Taurus Mountains   1514   Nakhichevan
×1516   Çaldiran   ×1554   Caspian
×1522   Marj Dabiq   Tabriz   Sea
Rhodes   Aleppo   1516   ×1514, 1534,
1555, 1585
Cyprus ×   SYRIA   ×Tehran
1571: captured from   Tripoli
Venetian Republic   ×1516   ×1534   Hamadan
Damascus   Baghdad
ria   ×1516   Jerusalem   Isfahan
Cairo   Al Raydaniyya
7   Suez   Basra   Zagros Mountains   SAFAVID
EMPIRE
YPT   ×1538   ×1551
Gombrun
to Portugal
HEJAZ   1554 ×   Persian Gulf
Bahrain
Medina   to Portugal   ×1551
Muscat   Tropic of Cancer   Muscat
to Portugal
Jedda   Arabian   OMAN
Mecca
Suakin   Peninsula

Massawa

FUNJ

ETHIOPIA   Socotra
1505: occupied by
Portuguese
500 km

500 miles   Aden   Gulf of Aden

139

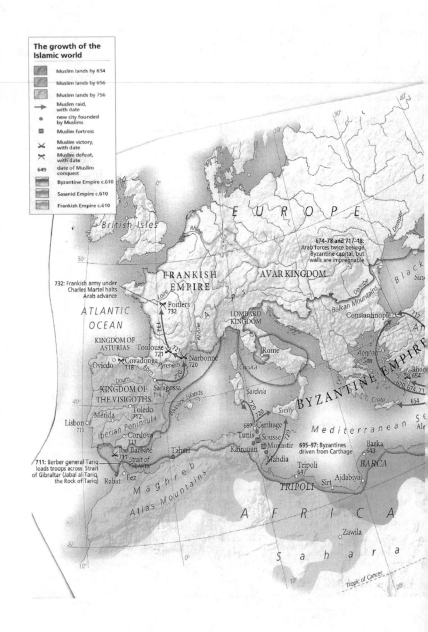

The growth of the Islamic world

Muslim lands by 634

Muslim lands by 656

Muslim lands by 756

→ Muslim raid, with date

● new city founded by Muslims

▩ Muslim fortress

✕ Muslim victory, with date

✕ Muslim defeat, with date

649 date of Muslim conquest

Byzantine Empire c.610

Sasanid Empire c.610

Frankish Empire c.610

EUROPE

British Isles

Rhine

FRANKISH EMPIRE

AVAR KINGDOM

674–78 and 717–18: Arab forces twice besiege Byzantine capital, but walls are impregnable

Danube

Balkan Mountains

Dniester

Black Sea

Constantinople

732: Frankish army under Charles Martel halts Arab advance

Loire

Alps

LOMBARD KINGDOM

ATLANTIC OCEAN

Poitiers 732

Rhône

Rome

KINGDOM OF ASTURIAS

Toulouse 721

721

Narbonne 720

Corsica

Aegean Sea

BYZANTINE EMPIRE

Oviedo ✕Covadonga 718

Pyrenees

720

Sardinia

Rhod 654

670 674, 71

Douro

Ebro

Saragossa 714

Balearic Islands

720

720

Sicily

Crete

654

KINGDOM OF THE VISIGOTHS

Toledo 712

Mérida

Lisbon 711

Iberian Peninsula

Cordova 711

697 Carthage

Tunis

Sousse

720

Mediterranean Se

Ale

711: Berber general Tariq leads troops across Strait of Gibraltar (Jabal al-Tariq, the Rock of Tariq)

Rio Barbate 711

Tahart

Strait of Gibraltar

Kairouan

Montastir

Mahdia

695–97: Byzantines driven from Carthage

Barka 643

BARCA

Fez

Rabat

Tripoli 647

Ajdabiya

Sirt

Maghreb

Atlas Mountains

TRIPOLI

AFRICA

Zawila

Sahara

Tropic of Cancer

Talas River
751

751: Arabs defeat
Chinese army and
stop Tang expansion
to the west

FERGHANA
Tang protectorate

A S I A

Syr Darya

Aral
Sea

Amu Darya

SOGDIANA   Samarkand

TRANSOXANIA

Bukhara   Balkh   Kabul

Hindu Kush

ZABULISTAN   Multan

KHAZAR
EMPIRE

Don

Kara Kum

Kandahar

Thar
Dese

Lashkari Bazar

Caspian Sea

Tus

Volga

KHURASAN   SISTAN

Gurgan

Caucasus   Tiflis

Qumis   Damghan   Nishapur   Herat

Iranian
Plateau   Kerman

ck Sea   Trebizond   ARMENIA   Ardabil   Qazvin   Nayin

Sinope   Theodosiopolis   647

Suleyman   TABARISTAN

Hamadan   SASANID   Yazd

Nehavend   EMPIRE   Isfahan
642   643   Susa

KERMAN

Malatya   Nineveh   Mosul   PERSIA   Niriz

Ankara   627   Zagros Mountains   FARS   Hormuz

Warash   MESOPOTAMIA   Shiraz

Anatolia   Adana   Samarra   Ana   KHUZISTAN   Siraf   Suhar   Muscat

RE   Tarsus   Raqqa   Al Madain   Euphrates   Basra

Homs 636   SYRIA   Baghdad   656

Rhodes   Cyprus   649   Damascus   Kerbela   Al Hira   BAHRAIN   Persian Gulf   OMAN

654   from 561: Umayyad capital   680   Kufa

24,717   654   Yarmuk   Qadisiya   Hasa

654   Pella   636   636

Amman

Jerusalem   Ainadain   NEJD   Yamama

Sea   638   634

Alexandria   Heliopolis
642   640

Al Fustat   Memphis   Tabuk   Mabiyyat   Arabian Sea

(Cairo)   641   Medina

EGYPT   HEJAZ   Arabian   Peninsula   Raysut

Nile   Badr
624

Jedda   Mecca
Ta'if   Socotra

Aswan   Najran   Shibam

Red Sea   Athr   YEMEN   Sana

Zabid   Aden

500 km

141

Books for Further Study and Muslim Sharing

The Meaning of The Holy Qur'an, by Abdullah Yusuf Ali
This is the very best translation of the Qur'an into English.
Gift of $25.00, includes postage.

Only Allah Can Give Real Peace, by Sylvain Romain
Pastor Romain is the Albanian Mission President. This is great to share
with your Muslim friends.
Gift of $5.00, or 10 copies for a gift of $30.00, includes postage.

Salvation in the Honored Qur'an, by Sylvain Romain
A wonderful follow-up book for your advanced Muslim friends. A must!
Gift of $5.00, or 10 copies for a gift of $30.00, includes postage.

Maroon Resource Book, compiled by Stephen Dickie
This book contains necessary information for the serious student
who wants to understand Islam in the light of unfolding Bible
prophecy. As we continue our research and understandings increase relevant to history, prophecy, and world events, additional
materials will be added to this book. Many of the source materials listed are not included in *Islam, God's Forgotten Blessing*.
Gift of $13.00 includes postage

OTHER BOOKS AVAILABLE

God's Healing Way, by Mary Ann McNeilus, MD
Priceless information about natural remedies and healthy lifestyle.
Gift of $12.00, includes postage.

The Ministry of Midwifery, Patti Barnes, CPM
A manual for midwives and childbirth education.
Gift of $15.00, includes postage.

Postage will be combined on multiple book orders to save you money
All prices are quoted as U. S. dollars based on 2006 costs, and shipped
within the United States of America. As prices increase, those costs will
be reflected accordingly. All book donations are requested to be made
by check or money order. Please include return address, clearly printed
or typed. All other book inquiries or any questions please contact:

Strawberry Meadow Association
P.O. Box 385
Kasson, MN 55944

(507) 633-1844 or sdickie@hotmail.com